What People Are Saying about Threshold Bible Study

"Threshold Bible Study is a wonderful series that helps modern people read the Bible with insight and joy. Each book highlights an important theme and helps us to hear and respond to God speaking to us in the Scriptures."

Richard J. Clifford, SJ, Professor of Biblical Studies
Weston Jesuit School of Theology, Cambridge, Massachusetts

"Stephen Binz's Threshold Bible Study is a marvelous project. With lucidity and creativity, Binz offers today's believing communities a rich and accessible treasury of biblical scholarship. The series' brilliance lies in its simplicity of presentation complemented by critical depth of thought and reflective insight. This is a wonderful gift for personal and communal study, especially for those wishing to make a home for the Word in their hearts."

Carol J. Dempsey, OP, Associate Professor of Theology
University of Portland, Oregon

"Threshold Bible Study offers a marvelous new approach for individuals and groups to study themes in our rich biblical and theological tradition. Moving through these thematic units feels like gazing at panels of stained glass windows, viewing similar images through different lights."

John Endres, SJ, Professor of Scripture
Jesuit School of Theology, Berkeley

"Threshold Bible Study provides an introduction to some major biblical themes, enabling Catholics to read, with greater understanding, the Bible in the Church. When studied along with the documents of Vatican II and the *Catechism of the Catholic Church*, this series can be a help for personal and group Bible study."

Francis Cardinal George, OMI, Archbishop of Chicago

"Threshold Bible Study offers solid scholarship and spiritual depth. Drawing on the Church's living Tradition and the Jewish roots of the New Testament, Threshold Bible Study can be counted on for lively individual study and prayer, even while it offers spiritual riches to deepen communal conversation and reflection among the people of God."

Scott Hahn, Professor of Biblical Theology, Franciscan University of Steubenville

"Threshold Bible Study is a refreshing approach to enable participants to ponder the Scriptures more deeply. The thematic material is clearly presented with a mix of information and spiritual nourishment. The questions are thoughtful and the principles for group discussion are quite helpful. This series provides a practical way for faithful people to get to know the Bible better and to enjoy the fruits of biblical prayer."

Irene Nowell, OSB, Mount St. Scholastica, Atchison, Kansas

"Threshold Bible Study is appropriately named, for its commentary and study questions bring people to the threshold of the text and invite them in. The questions guide but do not dominate. They lead readers to ponder and wrestle with the biblical passages and take them across the threshold toward life with God. Stephen Binz's work stands in the tradition of the biblical renewal movement and brings it back to life. We need more of this in the Church."

Kathleen M. O'Connor
Professor of Old Testament, Columbia Theological Seminary

"I most strongly recommend Stephen Binz's Threshold Bible Study for adult Bible classes, religious education, and personal spiritual enrichment. The series is exceptional for its scholarly solidity, pastoral practicality, and clarity of presentation. The Church owes Binz a great debt of gratitude for his generous and competent labor in the service of the Word of God."   Peter C. Phan, The Ignacio Ellacuria Professor of Catholic Social Thought

Georgetown University

"Threshold Bible Study is the perfect series of Bible study books for serious students with limited time. Each lesson is brief, illuminating, challenging, wittily written, and a pleasure to study. The reader will reap a rich harvest of wisdom from the efforts expended."

John J. Pilch, Adjunct Professor of Biblical Studies
Georgetown University, Washington, DC

"Threshold Bible Study unlocks the Scriptures and ushers the reader over the threshold into the world of God's living Word. The world of the Bible comes alive with new meaning and understanding for our times. This series enables the reader to appreciate contemporary biblical scholarship and the meaning of God's Word. This is the best material I have seen for serious Bible study."   Most Reverend Donald W. Trautman, Bishop of Erie

"Threshold Bible Study is that rare kind of program that will help one cross an elusive threshold—using the Bible effectively for prayer and spiritual enrichment. This user-friendly program will enhance any personal or group Bible study. Guaranteed to make your love of Scripture grow!"   Ronald D. Witherup, SS,

Biblical scholar and author of The Bible Companion

The
Feasts of Judaism

Stephen J. Binz

Fifth Printing 2015

Photos ©2006 Jack Hazut, www.israelimage.net

The Scripture passages contained herein are from the *New Revised Standard Version of the Bible*, Catholic edition. Copyright ©1989, by the Division of Christian Education of the National Council of Churches in the U.S.A. All rights reserved.

Twenty-Third Publications
A Division of Bayard
One Montauk Avenue, Suite 200
PO Box 6015
New London, CT 06320
(860)437-3012 or (800) 321-0411
www.23rdpublications.com

ISBN-10: 1-58595-596-5
ISBN 978-1-58595-596-1
Library of Congress Catalog Card Number: 2006902489

Contents

LESSONS 13–18

LESSONS 19–24

LESSONS 25–30

How to Use
Threshold Bible Study

Each book in the Threshold Bible Study series is designed to lead you through a new doorway of biblical awareness, to accompany you across a unique threshold of understanding. The characters, places, and images that you encounter in each of these topical studies will help you explore fresh dimensions of your faith and discover richer insights for your spiritual life.

Threshold Bible Study covers biblical themes in depth in a short amount of time. Unlike more traditional Bible studies that treat a biblical book or series of books, Threshold Bible Study aims to address specific topics within the entire Bible. The goal is not for you to comprehend everything about each passage, but rather for you to understand what a variety of passages from different books of the Bible reveals about the topic of each study.

Threshold Bible Study offers you an opportunity to explore the entire Bible from the viewpoint of a variety of different themes. The commentary that follows each biblical passage launches your reflection about that passage and helps you begin to see its significance within the context of your contemporary experience. The questions following the commentary challenge you to understand the passage more fully and apply it to your own life. The prayer starter helps conclude your study by integrating learning into your relationship with God.

These studies are designed for maximum flexibility. Each study is presented in a workbook format, with sections for reading, reflecting, writing, discussing, and praying. Space for writing after each question is ideal for personal study and allows group members to prepare in advance for their discussion. The thirty lessons in each topic may be used by an individual over the period of a month, or by a group for six sessions, with lessons to be studies each week before the next group meeting. These studies are ideal for Bible study groups, small Christian communities, adult faith formation, student groups, Sunday school, neighborhood groups, and family reading, as well as for individual learning.

The method of Threshold Bible Study is rooted in the classical tradition of *lectio divina*, an ancient yet contemporary means for reading the Scriptures reflectively and prayerfully. Reading and interpreting the text (*lectio*) is followed by reflective meditation on its message (*meditatio*). This reading and reflecting flows into prayer from the heart (*oratio* and *contemplatio*).

This ancient method assures us that Bible study is a matter of both the mind and the heart. It is not just an intellectual exercise to learn more and be able to discuss the Bible with others. It is, more importantly, a transforming experience. Reflecting on God's word, guided by the Holy Spirit, illumines the mind with wisdom and stirs the heart with zeal.

Following the personal Bible study, Threshold Bible Study offers a method for extending *lectio divina* into a weekly conversation with a small group. This communal experience will allow participants to enhance their appreciation of the message and build up a spiritual community (*collatio*). The end result will be to increase not only individual faith, but also faithful witness in the context of daily life (*operatio*).

Through the spiritual disciplines of Scripture reading, study, reflection, conversation, and prayer, you will experience God's grace more abundantly as your life is rooted more deeply in Christ. The risen Jesus said: "Listen! I am standing at the door, knocking; if you hear my voice and open the door, I will come in to you and eat with you, and you with me" (Rev 3:20). Listen to the Word of God, open the door, and cross the threshold to an unimaginable dwelling with God!

SUGGESTIONS FOR INDIVIDUAL STUDY

• Make your Bible reading a time of prayer. Ask for God's guidance as you read the Scriptures.

• Try to study daily, or as often as possible according to the circumstances of your life.

• Read the Bible passage carefully, trying to understand both its meaning and its personal application as you read. Some persons find it helpful to read the passage aloud.

• Read the passage in another Bible translation. Each version adds to your understanding of the original text.

• Allow the commentary to help you comprehend and apply the scriptural text. The commentary is only a beginning, not the last word on the meaning of the passage.

• After reflecting on each question, write out your responses. The very act of writing will help you clarify your thoughts, bring new insights, and amplify your understanding.

• As you reflect on your answers, think about how you can live God's word in the context of your daily life.

• Conclude each daily lesson by reading the prayer and continuing with your own prayer from the heart.

• Make sure your reflections and prayers are matters of both the mind and the heart. A true encounter with God's word is always a transforming experience.

• Choose a word or a phrase from the lesson to carry with you throughout the day as a reminder of your encounter with God's life-changing word.

• Share your learning experience with at least one other person whom you trust for additional insights and affirmation. The ideal way to share learning is in a small group that meets regularly.

SUGGESTIONS FOR GROUP STUDY

• Meet regularly; weekly is ideal. Try to be on time and make attendance a high priority for the sake of the group. The average group meets for about an hour.

• Open each session with a prepared prayer, a song, or a reflection. Find some appropriate way to bring the group from the workaday world into a sacred time of graced sharing.

• If you have not been together before, name tags are very helpful as a group begins to become acquainted with the other group members.

• Spend the first session getting acquainted with one another, reading the Introduction aloud, and discussing the questions that follow.

• Appoint a group facilitator to provide guidance to the discussion. The role of facilitator may rotate among members each week. The facilitator simply keeps the discussion on track; each person shares responsibility for the group. There is no need for the facilitator to be a trained teacher.

• Try to study the six lessons on your own during the week. When you have done your own reflection and written your own answers, you will be better prepared to discuss the six scriptural lessons with the group. If you have not had an opportunity to study the passages during the week, meet with the group anyway to share support and insights.

• Participate in the discussion as much as you are able, offering your thoughts, insights, feelings, and decisions. You learn by sharing with others the fruits of your study.

• Be careful not to dominate the discussion. It is important that everyone in the group be offered an equal opportunity to share the results of their work. Try to link what you say to the comments of others so that the group remains on the topic.

• When discussing your own personal thoughts or feelings, use "I" language. Be as personal and honest as appropriate and be very cautious about giving advice to others.

• Listen attentively to the other members of the group so as to learn from their insights. The words of the Bible affect each person in a different way, so a group provides a wealth of understanding for each member.

• Don't fear silence. Silence in a group is as important as silence in personal study. It allows individuals time to listen to the voice of God's Spirit and the opportunity to form their thoughts before they speak.

• Solicit several responses for each question. The thoughts of different people will build on the answers of others and will lead to deeper insights for all.

• Don't fear controversy. Differences of opinions are a sign of a healthy and honest group. If you cannot resolve an issue, continue on, agreeing to disagree. There is probably some truth in each viewpoint.

• Discuss the questions that seem most important for the group. There is no need to cover all the questions in the group session.

• Realize that some questions about the Bible cannot be resolved, even by experts. Don't get stuck on some issue for which there are no clear answers.

• Whatever is said in the group is said in confidence and should be regarded as such.

• Pray as a group in whatever way feels comfortable. Pray for the members of your group throughout the week.

Schedule for group study

Session 1: Introduction   Date: _____

Session 2: Lessons 1–6   Date: _____

Session 3: Lessons 7–12   Date: _____

Session 4: Lessons 13–18   Date: _____

Session 5: Lessons 19–24   Date: _____

Session 6: Lessons 25–30   Date: _____

These are the appointed festivals of the Lord, the holy convocations, which you shall celebrate at the time appointed for them. Lev 23:4

The Feasts of Judaism

Rabbi Abraham Joshua Heschel taught that the festivals of Judaism are the great cathedrals of the faith. Instead of creating material shrines, Judaism's sacred architecture consists of sanctuaries in time. He explains: "Judaism teaches us to be attached to holiness in time, to be attached to sacred events, to learn how to consecrate sanctuaries that emerge from the magnificent stream of a year." By creating an architecture of time, the Jewish people consecrate days within the cycle of weeks, months, seasons, and years in order to remember and celebrate the events and themes of the covenant.

The word "remember" is found throughout the Scriptures. The process of remembering God's saving deeds is not just a mental recall; remembering is active, tangible, and personal. The challenge of relating the past to the present is accomplished by appealing to the whole person: the mind, heart, and five senses. The feasts of the year enshrine the memories of what God has done and allow each new generation to participate in the effects of God's saving work. An old proverb says, "Put something where you can see it so your eye will remind your heart." Through the symbols, rituals, foods, and customs of the annual feasts, the Jewish people see, hear, smell, taste, and feel the living word of God.

Because the Jewish people created sanctuaries in time with their religious festivals, they produced something that the Babylonian conquerors, Roman armies, and German Nazis could not destroy. Repeating the Sabbath blessing every Friday evening, breaking the unleavened bread of the Seder, fasting in repentance on the Day of Atonement, lighting the candles of the Hanukkah menorah—these remembrances have played an essential role in unifying and preserving the Jewish people through the centuries in both joy and persecution. Children who participate in the family festivals sense that they belong to an ongoing tradition that has deep significance. The family and communal bonds created by the cycle of feasts build identity and security that gives life purpose and direction. With joy and thanksgiving, the feasts honor the Jewish tradition and pass on the experience of faith throughout the generations.

Reflection and discussion

• What feast of Judaism is most familiar to me? What do I know about that feast's traditions?

8 crazy nights!

• Why is tangible remembrance so necessary in building meaning and security in a person's life?

See it to believe it

Herman Wouk, in *This is My God*, wrote: "Time on earth is a pattern of wheels within wheels—the day, the week, the seasons, the year—and on each of the wheels Judaism has set its stamp."

The most deeply rooted of all Judaism's cycle of time is the weekly Sabbath. In the Genesis narrative, God blessed the seventh day and made it holy. Keeping the Sabbath has long been Israel's most important requirement for honoring the covenant and inclusion within the community. As a distinguishing mark of Judaism, Sabbath consists of a strictly regulated pause in the busy and burdensome routine of daily life. This weekly stoppage is not just a suggestion to better one's life with leisure; it is God's gift of emancipation in an anxiety-burdened world.

The Jewish year has twelve moon months of twenty-nine or thirty days. In biblical times, the day of the new moon, the first day of each lunar month, was a day of rejoicing and festivity, not only in Israel, but throughout the cultures of the Middle East. In ancient Israel, the new moon was a sign of God's fidelity and was celebrated with blowing trumpets, special sacrifices, ceasing from work, and festive meals (Num 10:10; Ps 81:3).

Three times a year the people of Israel celebrated pilgrimage feasts: the feast of Passover (Pesach), the feast of Weeks or Pentecost (Shavuot), and the feast of Booths or Tabernacles (Sukkot). During the period of the temple (until A.D. 70), these three feasts where characterized by pilgrimage to Jerusalem. The feasts of Passover and Booths began on the fifteenth day of their respective lunar months, when the moon is full—Passover in the spring (in our March-April) and Booths in the autumn (in our September-October). The feast of Weeks is celebrated seven weeks after Passover begins, falling on the fiftieth day after Passover (in our May-June).

These three feasts have both agricultural and historical significance. Agriculturally, Passover represents the beginning of the barley harvest in Israel. The feast of Weeks commemorates the time when the first fruits of the wheat were harvested and brought to the temple. The feast of Booths is a harvest festival marking the ripening of the grape and fruit crops and is sometimes referred to as the festival of ingathering. This annual tribute to the seasonal cycles of the earth is combined with the historical significance of the feasts. Passover remembers the exodus from Egypt after generations of slavery; Weeks celebrates the giving of the Torah at Mount Sinai; and Booths commemorates the forty-year period during which the children of Israel were wandering in the desert, living in temporary shelters, before entering the promised land.

The High Holy Days are the ten days starting with Rosh Hashanah, commonly known as the Jewish New Year, and ending with Yom Kippur, the Day of Atonement. These are days of serious introspection, a time to consider the sins of the previous year and to repent before God. Rosh Hashanah, occurring on the first day of the month of Tishri, is designated the festival of Trumpets in the Bible, and it is today marked by the sounding of the *shofar* (the ram's horn) in the synagogue. Yom Kippur is Judaism's most solemn day, a day of fasting, bowed heads, and wrung hearts. These Days of Awe fall in the first ten days of the lunar month in which the feast of Booths is celebrated.

The feasts that are not rooted in the Torah (the first five books of the Bible) are called minor holy days. The three most important of these minor, post-Mosaic feasts are the Ninth of Ab, Purim, and Hanukkah. The ninth day of the month of Ab marks the greatest disasters in Jewish history, the destruction of Jerusalem's first temple by the Babylonians and the destruction of the second temple by the Romans. It is marked with fasting, mourning customs, and readings from the book of Lamentations. Purim is a joyful holiday, rooted in the biblical story of Esther, a Jewish queen who saved her people from extermination in Persia. It is celebrated on the fourteenth day of Adar, a month before Passover begins (in our February-March). Hanukkah is an eight-day festival, also called the feast of Dedication. It celebrates the victory of the Maccabees over the Syrian ruler, Antiochus, and the rededication of the temple after its desecration. It is marked by the lighting of the eight candles of the Hanukkah menorah.

Reflection and discussion

• Our Hebrew ancestors associated the new moon with God's faithfulness and the full moon with the abundance of God's blessings. What do I associate with the waxing and waning of the moon?

• In what ways do I remember and celebrate the natural cycles and seasons of the year?

We have our own holiday traditions

The great feasts of Israel were occasions for renewing the covenant, for strengthening the bonds that held the Israelites together as the people of God. The annual cycle of festivals acknowledged God as the provider of his people and celebrated God's gracious gift of choosing the Israelites and personally delivering them. The physical expressions that characterized the feasts—processing, festive meals, singing, and dancing—were expressions of a lively religious faith and a heartfelt joy.

Israel's feasts were communal celebrations—the opposite of solitary piety. Everyone was involved, from the oldest to the youngest members of the community. Moses told the people to make sure no one was left out: "Rejoice during your festival, you and your sons and your daughters, your male and female slaves, as well as the Levites, the strangers, the orphans, and the widows resident in your towns" (Deut 16:14). The festivals are repeatedly called "holy convocations" (Lev 23:4), a time characterized by a break in life's ordinary routine, a time in which work was forbidden. The pilgrimage feasts involved travel from home and festivity with the whole community in Jerusalem. The most dramatic break from the routine was the feast of Booths, during which everyone camped out for seven days in huts covered with tree branches and leaves.

The biblical accounts of Israel's festivals are filled with ceremonies and rituals. Some of these were rites involving the whole community at the temple of Jerusalem; others were family rituals performed in the home. These symbols and rituals expressed an interior faith and taught the next generation how to live the faith of their ancestors. Teaching with words alone cannot compare to vivid actions like clearing the home of leaven, leaving a place setting for Elijah, marching with the palm branch, listening to the trumpet sound, and lighting the menorah. Carrying out the ceremonies of Israel's feasts over the course of a year can teach far more than can be learned in a classroom. The festival ceremonies expressed the living covenant, the active relationship between God and the community of faith.

During the era of the temple, most of the feasts were accompanied by either animal sacrifice or a harvest offering to God. These sacrifices and offerings were specifically prescribed in the Scriptures, for example: "You shall present with the bread seven lambs a year old without blemish, one young bull, and two rams; they shall be a burnt-offering to the Lord, along with their grain-offering and their drink-offerings, an offering by fire of pleasing odor to the Lord" (Lev 23:18). The sacrifices and offerings were exterior expressions of interior dispositions, a desire to return thanks to God for blessings received and to be forgiven and reconciled for offenses. Yet, there was no sharp line of demarcation between the spiritual and social dimensions of the festivals. The animals and grain offered to God also provided for a community meal. Although meat was relatively scarce in Israel's everyday life, it was noticeably present at most of the festivals, where the requirements of animal sacrifices insured a large banquet. Wine, also an expression of abundance and celebration, was in full evidence at the festivals.

Along with the solemnity of the festivals was the biblical commandment to "rejoice during your festival." The holy convocation was also a holiday filled with high spirits and the letting go of usual inhibitions. Isaiah describes the joy of the feast: "You shall have a song in the night when a holy festival is kept; and gladness of heart, as when one sets out to the sound of the flute to go to the mountain of the Lord" (Isa 30:29). Feasting, drinking, singing, dancing, and rejoicing—these are expressions of Israel's communal life in celebration of God's blessings.

The feasts celebrated by the Jewish people of today are diminished in their pomp and display from the lavishness of the festivals during the biblical period with its temple. The pilgrimage processions to Jerusalem, the radiantly decorated and crowded streets of the city, the glorious temple of the Lord, with its white-robed priests, fragrant sacrifices, and awesome solemnities are long-departed parts of an ancient past. Yet, the spirit of those feasts remains within contemporary Judaism, and the essence of those festivals are remembered in word and ritual in the homes and synagogues of Jewish people throughout the world. These sanctuaries in time consecrate the cycle of weeks, months, seasons, and years in order to enshrine for each generation the memories of what God has done.

Reflection and discussion

• In what way do the religious feasts of Israel express the whole person in relationship to God: refusing to separate the spiritual and physical, the sacrificial and social, solemnity and rejoicing?

• What can I learn about the joy of my religion through discovering the feasts of Israel?

From their roots in the Old Testament, these feasts also form the background for the New Testament. The festivals of Israel were at the heart of the religious life of Jesus. He went on pilgrimage to Jerusalem with his family and his disciples for the feasts of the Lord. He honored the Sabbath and celebrated the cycle of the year as he lived within the tradition of his Jewish ancestors.

Sometimes Christians believe that the Jewish feasts are no longer valid since Jesus proclaimed himself as Lord of the Sabbath and the gospels demonstrate that his saving deeds fulfilled the ancient feasts. Yet, Jesus taught that he had not come to abolish the Torah and that not one letter would pass from it until it is all accomplished (Matt 5:17–18). God's covenant with the Jewish people remains, for as Paul wrote, "the gifts and the calling of God are irrevocable" (Rom 11:29).

As Gentiles grafted onto the vine of Israel, we who are Christian are privileged to study the feasts of our elder brothers and sisters in Judaism. In Jesus, these festivals have become our heritage too. Learning the feasts of Judaism will enrich our understanding of the Scriptures, help us understand the roots of our tradition, and bring us closer to the faith of Jesus.

Reflection and discussion

• What are the main reasons I have been attracted to this study of the biblical feasts of Judaism?

• In what way can a study of the feasts of Judaism enrich my Christian faith?

Prayer

Lord God of Israel, you have created the heavenly bodies of sun and moon, and you have given us the rhythm of days, months, seasons, and years. We praise you for the cycles of fasting and feasting, mourning and rejoicing, struggle and celebration which mark our lives on earth. During this study of the biblical feasts of Judaism, give me a new respect and understanding for this part of my religious heritage, and lead me closer to the faith of Jesus. Guide, encourage, and enlighten me as I read and contemplate your inspired word.

SUGGESTIONS FOR FACILITATORS, GROUP SESSION 1

1. If the group is meeting for the first time, or if there are newcomers joining the group, it is helpful to provide nametags.

2. Distribute the books to the members of the group.

3. You may want to ask the participants to introduce themselves and tell the group a bit about themselves.

4. Ask one or more of these introductory questions:
   - What drew you to join this group?
   - What is your biggest fear in beginning this Bible study?
   - How is beginning this study like a "threshold" for you?

5. You may want to pray this prayer as a group:

Come upon us, Holy Spirit, to enlighten and guide us as we begin this study of the biblical feasts of Judaism. You marked the times and seasons of your chosen people with days of blessing, thanksgiving, and celebration. Motivate us to read the Scriptures and give us a deeper love for God's word each day. Work deeply within us so that your word, worship, and witness will be the foundations of our lives. Bless us during this session and throughout the coming week with the fire of your love.

6. Read the Introduction aloud, pausing at each question for discussion. Group members may wish to write the insights of the group as each question is discussed. Encourage several members of the group to respond to each question.

7. Don't feel compelled to finish the complete Introduction during the session. It is better to allow sufficient time to talk about the questions raised than to rush to the end. Group members may read any remaining sections on their own after the group meeting.

8. Instruct group members to read the first six lessons on their own during the six days before the next group meeting. They should write out their own answers to the questions as preparation for next week's group discussion.

9. Fill in the date for each group meeting under "Schedule for Group Study."

10. Conclude by praying aloud together the prayer at the end of the Introduction.

This day shall be a day of remembrance for you. You shall celebrate it as a festival to the Lord; throughout your generations you shall observe it as a perpetual ordinance. Exod 12:14

Instructions for the Feast of Passover

EXODUS 12:1–20 ¹*The Lord said to Moses and Aaron in the land of Egypt:* ²*This month shall mark for you the beginning of months; it shall be the first month of the year for you.* ³*Tell the whole congregation of Israel that on the tenth of this month they are to take a lamb for each family, a lamb for each household.* ⁴*If a household is too small for a whole lamb, it shall join its closest neighbor in obtaining one; the lamb shall be divided in proportion to the number of people who eat of it.* ⁵*Your lamb shall be without blemish, a year-old male; you may take it from the sheep or from the goats.* ⁶*You shall keep it until the fourteenth day of this month; then the whole assembled congregation of Israel shall slaughter it at twilight.* ⁷*They shall take some of the blood and put it on the two doorposts and the lintel of the houses in which they eat it.* ⁸*They shall eat the lamb that same night; they shall eat it roasted over the fire with unleavened bread and bitter herbs.* ⁹*Do not eat any of it raw or boiled in water, but roasted over the fire, with its head, legs, and inner organs.* ¹⁰*You shall let none of it remain until the morning; anything that remains until the morning you shall burn.* ¹¹*This is how you shall eat it: your loins girded,*

your sandals on your feet, and your staff in your hand; and you shall eat it hurried-
ly. It is the passover of the Lord. [12]*For I will pass through the land of Egypt that night,*
and I will strike down every firstborn in the land of Egypt, both human beings and
animals; on all the gods of Egypt I will execute judgments: I am the Lord. [13]*The*
blood shall be a sign for you on the houses where you live: when I see the blood, I
will pass over you, and no plague shall destroy you when I strike the land of Egypt.

[14]*This day shall be a day of remembrance for you. You shall celebrate it as a*
festival to the Lord; throughout your generations you shall observe it as a perpet-
ual ordinance. [15]*Seven days you shall eat unleavened bread; on the first day you*
shall remove leaven from your houses, for whoever eats leavened bread from the
first day until the seventh day shall be cut off from Israel. [16]*On the first day you*
shall hold a solemn assembly, and on the seventh day a solemn assembly; no
work shall be done on those days; only what everyone must eat, that alone may
be prepared by you. [17]*You shall observe the festival of unleavened bread, for on*
this very day I brought your companies out of the land of Egypt: you shall
observe this day throughout your generations as a perpetual ordinance. [18]*In the*
first month, from the evening of the fourteenth day until the evening of the twen-
ty-first day, you shall eat unleavened bread. [19]*For seven days no leaven shall be*
found in your houses; for whoever eats what is leavened shall be cut off from the
congregation of Israel, whether an alien or a native of the land. [20]*You shall eat*
nothing leavened; in all your settlements you shall eat unleavened bread.

Passover is first in the calendar of Jewish feasts, celebrated on the first full moon of springtime. It is the festival of redemption and freedom, honoring the beginning of Israel's existence as a free people.

Instructions for celebrating the Passover in future generations are woven through the biblical narrative of Israel's deliverance from the slavery of Egypt. God's instructions for what the Israelites were to do on the night of their liberation are joined with detailed prescriptions of how they are to cel-ebrate Passover in the years to come. In fact, the way the ritual was enacted through the centuries influenced the way the tradition was remembered and therefore the form in which it comes to us in the book of Exodus. In the memorial feast, the saving power of the past event became present again in the timeless event of the ritual. Past, present, and future generations come together on the night of Passover as the redeemed people of God.

The feasts of Passover and Unleavened Bread were originally separate nature festivals marking the new life of springtime. Passover is rooted in the days in which Israel's ancestors were nomadic shepherds. In the lunar month in which the lambs and kids were born, they observed a festival at full moon. The annual event was marked by the sacrifice of a sheep or goat from the flock and the sharing of the roasted animal by the whole family. The blood of the animal applied to their nomadic dwellings would bring God's favor and preserve them from harm in the year ahead.

During the period in which the Israelites were primarily farmers, their spring festival was related to the grain harvest. Before cutting the barley, they would get rid of all the fermented dough and old bread in order to celebrate the new harvest. On the first day of the feast of Unleavened Bread, the farmers would come in joyful procession to bring the first sheaf of their newly cut barley to the altar to be offered to God. All the people of the villages would then celebrate and give thanks in joyful feasting.

During the period of Israel's monarchy in Jerusalem, these two ancient festivals were merged into one great national feast centered at the temple. The ancient rituals took on new meaning and became a remembrance of God's redeeming power. The season of new life and nature's liberation became the season to celebrate the freedom of God's people and their awakening to new life. Passover recalled the time when God passed over the houses of the Israelites during the tenth plague—the death of the firstborn. Placing the blood of the lamb on the doorposts and lintel of the houses was the sign of God's redemption of his people. The unleavened bread called to mind the haste of the Israelite departure from Egypt, and the bitter herbs eaten with the sacrificial lamb recalled the bitterness of their former plight as slaves. Because the Lord passed over the houses of Israel during the tenth plague, Israel keeps Passover for the Lord.

Reflection and discussion

• What might be some reasons why Passover was celebrated on the first full moon of spring?

• Why are details of the Passover ritual woven throughout the historical narrative of Israel's escape from the slavery of Egypt?

• How do the sacrificed lamb and the unleavened bread recall earlier spring festivals?

• In what way are the foods of Passover powerful reminders of Israel's foundational event?

Prayer

God of Israel, you rescued your people from slavery and brought them into a life of freedom. Free me from all that prevents me from worshiping you and living the life to which you have called me.

That was for the Lord a night of vigil, to bring them out of the land of Egypt. That same night is a vigil to be kept for the Lord by all the Israelites throughout their generations. Exod 12:42

Keeping Vigil in Each Generation

EXODUS 12:21–42 ²¹ *Then Moses called all the elders of Israel and said to them, "Go, select lambs for your families, and slaughter the passover lamb. ²² Take a bunch of hyssop, dip it in the blood that is in the basin, and touch the lintel and the two doorposts with the blood in the basin. None of you shall go outside the door of your house until morning. ²³ For the Lord will pass through to strike down the Egyptians; when he sees the blood on the lintel and on the two doorposts, the Lord will pass over that door and will not allow the destroyer to enter your houses to strike you down. ²⁴ You shall observe this rite as a perpetual ordinance for you and your children. ²⁵ When you come to the land that the Lord will give you, as he has promised, you shall keep this observance. ²⁶ And when your children ask you, 'What do you mean by this observance?' ²⁷ you shall say, 'It is the passover sacrifice to the Lord, for he passed over the houses of the Israelites in Egypt, when he struck down the Egyptians but spared our houses.'" And the people bowed down and worshiped.*

²⁸ *The Israelites went and did just as the Lord had commanded Moses and Aaron.*

[29] *At midnight the Lord struck down all the firstborn in the land of Egypt, from the firstborn of Pharaoh who sat on his throne to the firstborn of the prisoner who was in the dungeon, and all the firstborn of the livestock.* [30] *Pharaoh arose in the night, he and all his officials and all the Egyptians; and there was a loud cry in Egypt, for there was not a house without someone dead.* [31] *Then he summoned Moses and Aaron in the night, and said, "Rise up, go away from my people, both you and the Israelites! Go, worship the Lord, as you said.* [32] *Take your flocks and your herds, as you said, and be gone. And bring a blessing on me too!"*

[33] *The Egyptians urged the people to hasten their departure from the land, for they said, "We shall all be dead."* [34] *So the people took their dough before it was leavened, with their kneading bowls wrapped up in their cloaks on their shoulders.* [35] *The Israelites had done as Moses told them; they had asked the Egyptians for jewelry of silver and gold, and for clothing,* [36] *and the Lord had given the people favor in the sight of the Egyptians, so that they let them have what they asked. And so they plundered the Egyptians.*

[37] *The Israelites journeyed from Rameses to Succoth, about six hundred thousand men on foot, besides children.* [38] *A mixed crowd also went up with them, and livestock in great numbers, both flocks and herds.* [39] *They baked unleavened cakes of the dough that they had brought out of Egypt; it was not leavened, because they were driven out of Egypt and could not wait, nor had they prepared any provisions for themselves.*

[40] *The time that the Israelites had lived in Egypt was four hundred thirty years.* [41] *At the end of four hundred thirty years, on that very day, all the companies of the Lord went out from the land of Egypt.* [42] *That was for the Lord a night of vigil, to bring them out of the land of Egypt. That same night is a vigil to be kept for the Lord by all the Israelites throughout their generations.*

The celebration of Israel's feasts combines the words of the Scriptures with the ritual actions prescribed therein. Rather than simply transmitting information about the past, this combination of narrative and ritual tells the story in a way that creates the experience anew. The elder of each family tells the familiar story of Passover and leads the memorable ritual to transmit the tradition to his children. In this way every generation will keep the Passover for God and experience God's saving deed for their people.

The biblical text takes it for granted that the children in each generation will ask questions about the meaning of the Passover observance (verse 26). Every good parent and teacher knows that children are open to learning new things only when they have questions to be answered. So the secret to educating the next generation is to help them generate good questions. The Jewish family ritual of Passover presents symbolic foods and actions which raise questions in the minds of the children. This creates an eager audience and prevents the narrative from being a predictable repetition. In the traditional ritual, the youngest child asks, "Why is this night different from all other nights?" The questions create the interest so that the story of Israel's night of liberation can be told. The technique has worked for millennia. Few Jewish children are raised without knowing the story of the exodus and feeling that it is an intimate part of their own history.

When the ancient Israelites celebrated Passover, they dramatically applied the blood of the slain lamb to the entrance of each home. In Israel's sacrificial tradition, the blood represents life (Lev 17:11), and the blood of the lamb identified God's people so that God would save them from death. The promise of God together with the lamb's blood, God's word and God's deed, bring about redemption.

What God did for the Israelites on the night of Passover, he does for every generation. Every human heart desires freedom and God desires to give the fullness of life to all people. The biblical texts remind us that God's redemption is not just for the chosen few, but ultimately for the entire world. The redemption of God's people on the night of Passover anticipates the fulfillment of God's promises to make Israel a blessing to all the communities of the earth.

The night of Passover is described as a night of vigil (verse 42), a time of careful watching. God kept his commitment to carefully watch over Israel on this death-filled night and bring her to freedom. Now Israel must keep the commitment of Passover, "a vigil to be kept for the Lord by all the Israelites throughout their generations." What God did for the Israelites is paralleled by their careful observance of Passover. This night of watching is a time of remembering the past and anticipating the future that God will bring. The suddenness of Israel's night of liberation in the past reminds future generations that God acts unexpectedly and that God's people must always live in vigilant expectation.

Reflection and discussion

• In what way does the Passover celebration create the experience anew in each generation?

• How does the feast generate questions within children and motivate them to learn their tradition?

• In what way does the Jewish Passover encourage me to live my life in careful watching for God's next move?

Prayer

God of freedom and life, you desire our liberation from all that prevents us from living fully. May I live my life in watchful expectancy, waiting for the fulfillment of all your promises. Help me to hope in your assurances and trust in your faithfulness.

You shall tell your child on that day, "It is because of what the Lord did for me when I came out of Egypt." Exod 13:8

Remember the Day of Your Liberation

EXODUS 12:43—13:10 ⁴³*The Lord said to Moses and Aaron: This is the ordinance for the passover: no foreigner shall eat of it, ⁴⁴but any slave who has been purchased may eat of it after he has been circumcised; ⁴⁵no bound or hired servant may eat of it. ⁴⁶It shall be eaten in one house; you shall not take any of the animal outside the house, and you shall not break any of its bones. ⁴⁷The whole congregation of Israel shall celebrate it. ⁴⁸If an alien who resides with you wants to celebrate the passover to the Lord, all his males shall be circumcised; then he may draw near to celebrate it; he shall be regarded as a native of the land. But no uncircumcised person shall eat of it; ⁴⁹there shall be one law for the native and for the alien who resides among you.*

⁵⁰All the Israelites did just as the Lord had commanded Moses and Aaron. ⁵¹That very day the Lord brought the Israelites out of the land of Egypt, company by company.

13 ³*Moses said to the people, "Remember this day on which you came out of Egypt, out of the house of slavery, because the Lord brought you out from there*

by strength of hand; no leavened bread shall be eaten. ⁴Today, in the month of Abib, you are going out. ⁵When the Lord brings you into the land of the Canaanites, the Hittites, the Amorites, the Hivites, and the Jebusites, which he swore to your ancestors to give you, a land flowing with milk and honey, you shall keep this observance in this month. ⁶Seven days you shall eat unleavened bread, and on the seventh day there shall be a festival to the Lord. ⁷Unleavened bread shall be eaten for seven days; no leavened bread shall be seen in your possession, and no leaven shall be seen among you in all your territory. ⁸You shall tell your child on that day, 'It is because of what the Lord did for me when I came out of Egypt.' ⁹It shall serve for you as a sign on your hand and as a reminder on your forehead, so that the teaching of the Lord may be on your lips; for with a strong hand the Lord brought you out of Egypt. ¹⁰You shall keep this ordinance at its proper time from year to year."

The experience of redemption is an ongoing, living reality for God's people. The faithfulness of the Israelites in observing the Passover is intimately united with God's action in bringing about their deliverance (verses 50-51). Through the instrument of human obedience and fidelity, God works salvation. Through the close joining of the book of Exodus and the feast of Passover, the experience of liberation and deliverance continues to be a reality for God's people from age to age.

The biblical text indicates that God's saving power, manifested at the time of the exodus, continues to be experienced as each generation celebrates the Passover. Moses' command to remember (verse 3) is not just a matter of recalling something that happened in the past. Through the rituals of Passover, God's people remember their past in a way that makes it real in the present. The people of each generation are to celebrate Passover in a way that helps them feel that they themselves were redeemed from slavery. Exodus is not just a story about Israel's ancestors, it is what God does for the individuals of every age. As Moses said, "You shall tell your children on that day, 'It is because of what the Lord did for me when I came out of Egypt'" (verse 8). Through the replication of the events of that original night, each person experiences a personal liberation from bondage. The words of the biblical text and the rituals of the Passover become the sacramental vehicles through which God brings about salvation for each new generation.

Israel's memory is a physical and bodily experience. Passover is a tangible sign and a concrete reminder. Moses declared that the whole person—through gestures, words, and rituals—would express God's saving deeds: "It shall serve for you as a sign on your hand and as a reminder on your forehead, so that the teaching of the Lord may be on your lips" (verse 9). Through the interweaving of past and present, the involvement of children, and the use of sacramental symbols, the ritual incorporates new generations into the experience of the exodus.

For the Jewish people and all who share in their heritage, Egypt is not a place that was left only once; it is a place to be left continually. Egypt represents not only physical or political bondage, but personal and spiritual imprisonment as well. To celebrate Passover is to be freed from internal confinement, narrow mindedness, and apathetic hopelessness. It is a liberation that has not fully happened yet, but that is always happening whenever people enter into the event.

To tell the story of Exodus in the context of the feast of Passover is to believe in the liberation to come. The memory of slavery evokes feelings of repulsion and determination to help others escape that state. Children must be involved in celebrating Passover for it is essential that they join in the unfinished work of liberation. Passover impels every generation to enter into the task of the covenant with God, the redemption of humanity.

Reflection and discussion

• In what ways does Moses' command to "remember" express the meaning of Passover? For the feasts of Judaism, what is the difference between remembering and recalling?

• What are the broad meanings of Egypt, slavery, and freedom in the context of contemporary Jewish experience? How does the Jewish tradition indicate that redemption and liberation are lifelong, ongoing realities?

• In what way are the five senses involved in the Passover remembrance? Why is this such an effective way to teach?

• From what types of bondage do people need to experience liberation today? What can I do to continue the experience of Exodus in my life today?

Prayer

Liberating Lord, you desire freedom and redemption for all your people. Through reflecting on your liberating action in the past, give me the desire to live in freedom and the commitment to work for the deliverance of others.

You shall offer the passover sacrifice for the Lord your God, from the flock and the herd, at the place that the Lord will choose as a dwelling for his name. Deut 16:2

Sacrifice in the Temple of Jerusalem

DEUTERONOMY 16:1–8 ¹*Observe the month of Abib by keeping the passover for the Lord your God, for in the month of Abib the Lord your God brought you out of Egypt by night.* ²*You shall offer the passover sacrifice for the Lord your God, from the flock and the herd, at the place that the Lord will choose as a dwelling for his name.* ³*You must not eat with it anything leavened. For seven days you shall eat unleavened bread with it—the bread of affliction—because you came out of the land of Egypt in great haste, so that all the days of your life you may remember the day of your departure from the land of Egypt.* ⁴*No leaven shall be seen with you in all your territory for seven days; and none of the meat of what you slaughter on the evening of the first day shall remain until morning.* ⁵*You are not permitted to offer the passover sacrifice within any of your towns that the Lord your God is giving you.* ⁶*But at the place that the Lord your God will choose as a dwelling for his name, only there shall you offer the passover sacrifice, in the evening at sunset, the time of day when you departed from Egypt.* ⁷*You shall cook it and eat it at the place that the Lord your God* *will choose; the next morning you may go back to your tents. ⁸For six days you shall continue to eat unleavened bread, and on the seventh day there shall be a solemn assembly for the Lord your God, when you shall do no work.*

The Torah emphasizes that Passover occurs in the springtime. In biblical times, the month in which the holiday fell was called Abib (verse 1), which means "new ears of grain." After the exile, the lunar months were given Babylonian names and Passover's month was renamed Nisan, the name that is still in use today. Because the twelve lunar months add up to only 354 days, and the solar year consists of about 365 days, the Jewish calendar periodically adds an extra month so that Passover always falls in the springtime (in our March-April). If the new ears of grain have not appeared after the month of Adar, an additional month (Adar II) is added to the year so that the month of Passover always begins when the immature ears of grain have begun to grow on the stalk.

By maintaining a close connection between the springtime and the liberation of Exodus, the Jewish tradition verifies that both nature and history confirm the triumph of life over death. Life blossoming, breaking the death grip of winter, parallels the human yearning for liberation and new life. In the Passover, biblical language and symbol point to spring as nature's counterpart to human redemption. The holy rhythm of Israel's life remains in tune with nature's cycles.

The text emphasizes Passover as one of Israel's three pilgrimage feasts, a festival requiring travel to Jerusalem and its temple. Set in the context of Israel's exodus, Deuteronomy refers to the temple that would be built in Jerusalem as "the place that the Lord will choose as a dwelling for his name" (verse 2). Prior to the establishment of the single chosen sanctuary in Jerusalem, the festival was celebrated in any of the various shrines throughout Israel's tribal confederation (verse 5). But from the time of the consolidation of all worship and sacrifice in Jerusalem until the temple's destruction in A.D. 70, the festival of Passover was marked by the procession of families from throughout the land traveling up to Jerusalem.

Deuteronomy's description of the festival still indicates the remnants of two distinct institutions, the Passover sacrifice offered at the temple and the seven-day feast of unleavened bread. Yet, both are combined into a single celebration of liberation: the sacrifice commemorating God's deliverance of Israel from slavery in Egypt (verse 6) and eating unleavened bread as a remembrance of the haste of their departure (verse 3). Only the first day of the feast had to be celebrated in Jerusalem; the remaining six days could be celebrated in their hometowns, culminating in a holiday free from work on the seventh day (verses 7–8).

The prohibition of work on the days of Israel's feasts was not interpreted as strictly as the Sabbath prohibition. The specifications in the book of Exodus allow for the preparation of food on those days: "On the first day you shall hold a solemn assembly, and on the seventh day a solemn assembly; no work shall be done on those days; only what everyone must eat, that alone may be prepared by you" (Exod 12:16). The rabbis interpreted this passage to apply to all the feasts so that the leisure of the holiday is enforced but food may be prepared for celebration. Good food is a necessity for joyful festivity.

Reflection and discussion

• Why is it important that the Jewish calendar be periodically adjusted so that Passover falls in the spring?

• What is the relationship in Israel's historical memory between eating the Passover sacrifice and eating unleavened bread?

Prayer

Lord God, you are the Creator of nature's seasons and the Redeemer of your people. Through the annual cycle of winter to spring, help me to rejoice in the triumph of love over oppression, freedom over bondage, and life over death.

The people of Israel who were present at Jerusalem kept the festival of unleavened bread seven days with great gladness; and the Levites and the priests praised the Lord day by day, accompanied by loud instruments for the Lord. 2 Chron 30:21

The Festival of Unleavened Bread

2 CHRONICLES 30:13–22 [13]*Many people came together in Jerusalem to keep the festival of unleavened bread in the second month, a very large assembly.* [14]*They set to work and removed the altars that were in Jerusalem, and all the altars for offering incense they took away and threw into the Wadi Kidron.* [15]*They slaughtered the passover lamb on the fourteenth day of the second month. The priests and the Levites were ashamed, and they sanctified themselves and brought burnt offerings into the house of the Lord.* [16]*They took their accustomed posts according to the law of Moses the man of God; the priests dashed the blood that they received from the hands of the Levites.* [17]*For there were many in the assembly who had not sanctified themselves; therefore the Levites had to slaughter the passover lamb for everyone who was not clean, to make it holy to the Lord.* [18]*For a multitude of the people, many of them from Ephraim, Manasseh, Issachar, and Zebulun, had not cleansed themselves, yet they ate the passover otherwise than as prescribed. But Hezekiah prayed for them, saying, "The good Lord pardon all* [19]*who set their hearts* *to seek God, the Lord the God of their ancestors, even though not in accordance with the sanctuary's rules of cleanness." *[20]*The Lord heard Hezekiah, and healed the people. *[21]*The people of Israel who were present at Jerusalem kept the festival of unleavened bread seven days with great gladness; and the Levites and the priests praised the Lord day by day, accompanied by loud instruments for the Lord. *[22]*Hezekiah spoke encouragingly to all the Levites who showed good skill in the service of the Lord. So the people ate the food of the festival for seven days, sacrificing offerings of well-being and giving thanks to the Lord the God of their ancestors.*

A great reform movement was initiated during the reign of King Hezekiah, following the treacherous reign of his predecessor, King Ahaz, who closed the temple and set up altars to foreign gods throughout Jerusalem. Hezekiah purified the temple, destroyed the altars of pagan worship, and reinstituted the feasts of Israel, beginning with Passover and the feast of Unleavened Bread. A provision in the Torah allowed for celebrating Passover one month late if a worshiper is ritually unclean or is traveling (Num 9:9–11). Because of the corruption of the whole nation under Ahaz, this provision was extended to the whole population. Since the temple had not been cleansed and the priests not yet sanctified during the first month, the festival was held in the second month (verse 13-15).

Like springtime, Passover is the opportunity to begin again. The celebration of the feast, with the great numbers who came to Jerusalem, reunited the people of the divided kingdom around the ancient traditions. Worshiping together under the reforms of Hezekiah joined the people into one faith and one purpose. Since right worship inspires and empowers right action, the renewed celebration of the feast led to the ongoing reform of the nation.

The Levites slaughtered the Passover lamb for each family group and the priests then dashed the sacrificial blood upon the altar as prescribed for sacrifices in the book of Leviticus. By this period of history, the blood was no longer placed on the entrance of each individual home, as prescribed for the exodus. Rather the blood splashed upon the altar of the temple expressed God's redemption of the whole people.

Many of the people who had come to Jerusalem for the first time in many generations had not properly sanctified and purified themselves "in accordance with the sanctuary's rules of cleanliness" (verse 18-19). But Hezekiah prayed for their pardon because the people had "set their hearts to seek God, the Lord of their ancestors." According to this text, as well as many teachings of the biblical prophets and the rabbis of Judaism, the most important requirement of proper worship is the disposition of the heart. Though the people were unable to fulfill all the laws of ritual purity, God healed the people (verse 20) because of the prayers of Hezekiah and the quality of their hearts. The people of Israel, then, ate the Passover meal and kept the festival with joy and thanksgiving.

This great festival of faith under Hezekiah is the first pilgrimage feast actually described in the Bible. A distinction is still made between the one-day Passover, on the fourteenth day of the month, and the seven-day festival of Unleavened Bread. Following the Passover, the people continued to celebrate "with great gladness" (verse 21), praising God each day with liturgical music and eating "the food of the festival for seven days" (verse 22).

Celebrating the exodus from Egypt and rejoicing in the fertility of the promised land were never separated; the historical memories and the agricultural feasts were always integral parts of Israel's national story. The unleavened bread is both a historical memory of the rush to leave Egypt and a celebration of the new crop of grain. As such, it represents a new beginning in every springtime.

In contemporary Judaism, a thorough housecleaning is done each year in preparation for Passover. Every speck of *hametz* (any food made with yeast or leaven) must be removed from the house before sitting down to the Passover meal. Leaven has come to symbolize any type of arrogance, self-indulgence, or self-assertion. The Jewish people focus on ridding themselves of this spiritual hametz before Passover as they also rid their homes of any remaining bits of leavened products. This absence of leaven is expressed by baking *matzah*, the flat, unleavened bread of Passover. The eating of leaven is forbidden and only matzah is eaten with the meals of the seven-day feast in order to give honor to God for the new crop of grain and in memory of God's hasty deliverance of his people from slavery.

Reflection and discussion

• Why was Passover the first feast celebrated in the newly purified temple? In what way does Passover express new beginnings?

• What does the fact that "the people ate the Passover otherwise than as prescribed" (verse 18–19) tell me about what God desires most (see Mic 6:8)?

• What are some of the reasons why only unleavened bread is eaten during the seven days of the feast?

Prayer

Lord God, you renew your people in every age and give us numerous opportunities to begin again. Help me to rid my life of all that inflates myself to the detriment of others and to cleanse my life of all unfaithfulness. Let me begin my life again in covenant with you.

Go into the city to a certain man, and say to him,
"The Teacher says, My time is near; I will keep the Passover at your house
with my disciples." Matt 26:18

Jesus' Passover Supper and Sacrifice

MATTHEW 26:17–30 [17]*On the first day of Unleavened Bread the disciples came to Jesus, saying, "Where do you want us to make the preparations for you to eat the Passover?"* [18]*He said, "Go into the city to a certain man, and say to him, 'The Teacher says, My time is near; I will keep the Passover at your house with my disciples.'"* [19]*So the disciples did as Jesus had directed them, and they prepared the Passover meal.*

[20]*When it was evening, he took his place with the twelve;* [21]*and while they were eating, he said, "Truly I tell you, one of you will betray me."* [22]*And they became greatly distressed and began to say to him one after another, "Surely not I, Lord?"* [23]*He answered, "The one who has dipped his hand into the bowl with me will betray me.* [24]*The Son of Man goes as it is written of him, but woe to that one by whom the Son of Man is betrayed! It would have been better for that one not to have been born."* [25]*Judas, who betrayed him, said, "Surely not I, Rabbi?" He replied, "You have said so."*

[26]*While they were eating, Jesus took a loaf of bread, and after blessing it he broke it, gave it to the disciples, and said, "Take, eat; this is my body."* [27]*Then he took a cup, and after giving thanks he gave it to them, saying, "Drink from it, all of you;* [28]*for this is my blood of the covenant, which is poured out for many for*

the forgiveness of sins. ²⁹*I tell you, I will never again drink of this fruit of the vine until that day when I drink it new with you in my Father's kingdom."*

³⁰*When they had sung the hymn, they went out to the Mount of Olives.*

During the time of Judaism's Second Temple period, which includes the life of Jesus, the ritual of Passover was a combination of the ancient Passover that was observed in the home and the Passover of Israel's monarchy that was observed only in the temple. Passover during this Second Temple period was divided into two main parts. In the afternoon before Passover began, the sacrificial lamb was slain with elaborate ceremonies in the temple; it was then brought home, roasted, and eaten in groups according to a ritual similar to the Jewish Seder of today. Outside the vicinity of Jerusalem, Jews would celebrate Passover in their home and synagogue, omitting the sacrifice of the lamb.

In the century before the temple's destruction in A.D. 70, when the Jews suffered under the heavy oppression of the Romans, Passover flamed the Jewish hope of the Messiah's coming. They knew that the coming messianic deliverance would be manifested with even greater miracles than God performed in redeeming his people from Egypt. The Messiah would be a new Moses, freeing the Jews at Passover, just as their ancestors were released from slavery.

Contained within the original salvation from Egypt are the seeds of future redemption. Passover had become the feast of watching for God's final redemption, "a vigil to be kept for the Lord by all the Israelites throughout their generations" (Exod 12:42). With every inn and guestroom filled to overflowing, and with thousands of people camping in the areas around the city, Jerusalem was never so crowded. With Jews from near and far and from every country to which Jews had wandered converging on Jerusalem, and with thoughts of being released from bondage on their minds, the feast was a potentially explosive time. For this reason, the Roman governor came to Jerusalem during the days of Passover along with a large contingent of Roman troops to supervise the crowds.

At the Last Passover of Jesus, he faced the same problem as all the pilgrims—finding a place to eat the meal and making arrangements for all the elements of the meal. Because of the requirement that the lamb be roasted whole and eaten completely on that same night, Jews gathered in groups of ten or more people, enough to consume the entire lamb. At mid-afternoon, amid blasts of the trumpets, the lambs were slain at the temple, and as darkness descended, the lambs were roasted and eaten. Dressed in festive clothes, the pilgrims began the ritual of the Passover meal as the full moon shone over the city.

Jesus ate the meal at a home with his disciples, not seated in chairs but reclining on cushions, as was the custom. He led the ceremonial observance, interpreting the details of the meal with great attention to the cups of wine, the matzah, and the bitter herbs. He looked backward gratefully at God's saving actions in the past and looked forward to the redemption to come. The betrayal of Judas is all the more tragic because it is done in the context of the bond created by the Passover meal. At the feast that celebrates Jewish freedom and their union with God, Judas uses his freedom to make a dreadful choice, severing his union with Christ and his responsibilities in the new covenant.

Jesus took the matzah in his hands and broke it, reciting the traditional Jewish blessing. Then giving it to his disciples he said, "Take, eat; this is my body." Holding the cup of red wine, representing the blood of the Passover shed for Israel's redemption, Jesus delivered the traditional prayer of thanksgiving. Then giving it to his disciples he said, "Drink from it, all of you; for this is my blood of the covenant." Jesus interpreted the Passover elements as his broken body and his blood poured out, his own Passover sacrifice for redemption and the forgiveness of sins. His own saving death would be the definitive covenant renewal and the affirmation of God's desire to bring his people the fullness of liberation in God's kingdom (verse 29).

The meal ended as Jesus and his disciples sang Hallel (verse 30), Psalms 113–118, proclaiming God's faithfulness and redeeming power. Jesus went out with his disciples to the Mount of Olives, which would have served as a campground for the large crowds unable to find lodging within the walls of the city. There in the moonlit night, in the tradition of his ancestors, Jesus would keep vigil for the Lord on this night of watching.

After the destruction of the temple in A.D. 70, when the gospel of Matthew was written, all Jews faced the critical issue of how to celebrate Passover now that pilgrimage to Jerusalem and the sacrifice of lambs in the temple were no longer possible. The rabbis transformed the domestic sacrificial meal into a non-sacrificial Seder meal, the narrated, symbolic ritual celebrated in Jewish homes today. The Jewish Christians of Matthew's community expressed the death and resurrection of Jesus in terms of the primary themes of Passover and continued to experience the fruit of that saving event in the Christian Eucharist.

Reflection and discussion

• In what way does Passover look both to the past and to the future?

• Why is an understanding of the Jewish Passover so necessary to interpret the meaning of Jesus' Passion?

• What aspects of the Christian Eucharist are rooted in the Jewish Passover? What is the evidence of their common origins?

Prayer

Father of Jesus, on the night of Passover you saved your people from slavery and death. Through the broken body of your Son and through his blood poured out for us, free me from bondage to sin and evil. Help me trust in your promise to bring me the fullness of salvation and life in your kingdom.

SUGGESTIONS FOR FACILITATORS, GROUP SESSION 2

1. If there are newcomers who were not present for the first group session, introduce them now.

2. You may want to pray this prayer as a group:

Lord God of our ancestors, your greatest desire is to free your people from bondage and enable them to experience new life. Through our study of the ancient feast of Passover, help us to understand more fully how you work through the cycles of nature and intervene in your people's history to always give us new hope. As we reflect on the traditions of the past, give us the desire to overcome oppression, bondage, sin, and apathy, so that we can be instruments of your liberating work in the world.

3. Ask one or more of the following questions:

- What was your biggest challenge in Bible study over this past week?
- What did you learn about yourself this week?

4. Discuss lessons 1 through 6 together. Assuming that group members have read the Scripture and commentary during the week, there is no need to read it aloud. As you review each lesson, you might want to briefly summarize the Scripture passages of each lesson and ask the group what stands out most clearly from the commentary.

5. Choose one or more of the questions for reflection and discussion from each lesson to talk over as a group. You may want to ask group members which question was most challenging or helpful to them as you review each lesson.

6. Keep the discussion moving, but don't rush the discussion in order to complete more questions. Allow time for the questions that provoke the most discussion.

7. Instruct group members to complete lessons 7 through 12 on their own during the six days before the next group meeting. They should write out their own answers to the questions as preparation for next week's group discussion.

8. Conclude by praying aloud together the prayer at the end of lesson 6, or any other prayer you choose.

You shall count seven weeks; begin to count the seven weeks from the time the sickle is first put to the standing grain. Then you shall keep the festival of weeks for the Lord your God. Deut 16:9–10

Keeping the Festival of the Weeks

LEVITICUS 23:15–22 *¹⁵And from the day after the sabbath, from the day on which you bring the sheaf of the elevation-offering, you shall count off seven weeks; they shall be complete. ¹⁶You shall count until the day after the seventh sabbath, fifty days; then you shall present an offering of new grain to the Lord. ¹⁷You shall bring from your settlements two loaves of bread as an elevation-offering, each made of two-tenths of an ephah; they shall be of choice flour, baked with leaven, as first fruits to the Lord. ¹⁸You shall present with the bread seven lambs a year old without blemish, one young bull, and two rams; they shall be a burnt-offering to the Lord, along with their grain-offering and their drink-offerings, an offering by fire of pleasing odor to the Lord. ¹⁹You shall also offer one male goat for a sin-offering, and two male lambs a year old as a sacrifice of well-being. ²⁰The priest shall raise them with the bread of the first fruits as an elevation-offering before the Lord, together with the two lambs; they shall be holy to the Lord for the priest. ²¹On that same day you shall make proclamation; you shall hold a holy convocation; you shall not work at your occupations. This is a statute for ever in all your settlements throughout your generations.*

²²When you reap the harvest of your land, you shall not reap to the very edges of your field, or gather the gleanings of your harvest; you shall leave them for the poor and for the alien: I am the Lord your God.

DEUTERONOMY 16:9–12 *⁹You shall count seven weeks; begin to count the seven weeks from the time the sickle is first put to the standing grain. ¹⁰Then you shall keep the festival of weeks for the Lord your God, contributing a freewill offering in proportion to the blessing that you have received from the Lord your God. ¹¹Rejoice before the Lord your God—you and your sons and your daughters, your male and female slaves, the Levites resident in your towns, as well as the strangers, the orphans, and the widows who are among you—at the place that the Lord your God will choose as a dwelling for his name. ¹²Remember that you were a slave in Egypt, and diligently observe these statutes.*

The feast of Weeks (Shavuot), the second of the three pilgrimage feasts of ancient Israel, was originally an agricultural festival. It is celebrated seven weeks—a week of weeks—after Passover (in our May-June). Because the counting period began on the second evening of Passover, the feast of Weeks takes place exactly fifty days after the Passover meal. Hence, the feast is also called Pentecost, from the Greek word for fifty.

In this way, the feasts of Weeks is related to Passover, with the two feasts marking both the beginning and the end of the grain harvest. In the days of the temple, the pilgrims at Passover brought a measure (called an omer) of their newly cut barley to the altar for a ceremony hailing the earth's newly awakened fertility. From the day the offering of barley was brought to the temple, seven full weeks were counted off (called "the counting of the omer"), the time required for the other grains to mature. On the fiftieth day, Israel celebrated its summer festival, the feast of Weeks, and pilgrims once more poured into Jerusalem, bringing the first fruits of their wheat harvest. This offering was two leavened loaves of bread, baked with the wheat of the new crop.

In time, the feast of Weeks took on a new historical significance in relationship to the exodus and new spiritual content. Beginning in the Second Temple period, the sages calculated that the Israelites arrived at Sinai at the beginning of the third month after their departure from Egypt (Exod 19:1) and that they received the gift of the Torah from God on the fiftieth day after Passover. With this new significance, the feast of Weeks marked the annual anniversary of God's covenant with Israel and the birthday of the Torah.

This counting of the seven weeks, from the sixteenth of Nisan (the second day of Passover) until the feast of Weeks, served to connect the anniversary of the exodus from Egypt with the festival that commemorates the giving of the Torah at Mount Sinai. Jewish tradition holds that God announced to the Israelites in Egypt that the Torah would be given to them fifty days after the exodus. As soon as they were liberated, they were so eager for the arrival of God's gift that they began to count the days. Thus, the counting of the days between Passover and Shavuot symbolizes the eagerness with which the Torah was received by the Israelites.

It is customary to decorate homes and synagogues with greenery and flowers for the feast. A colorful tradition states that the desert of Sinai became green and sprouted flowers in honor of God's Torah. The traditional foods of the feast, especially cheese blintzes, are made of dairy products, because the Torah is often compared to sweet milk and honey. Jewish mysticism describes God as a groom and Israel as his bride. Shavuot, say the mystics, is the anniversary of the marriage between God and Israel. The mystics also say that the two loaves of bread offered on the feast mirror its spiritual harvest, the two tablets of God's commandments.

The biblical book most associated with the feast is Ruth. The story takes place during the harvest associated with the holiday. The Moabite woman, Ruth, was the exemplary convert to Judaism, joyfully taking on its laws and traditions just as the Jews accepted God's Torah. She asserted the rights of the poor to glean the leftovers from the harvest, and through her marriage to Boaz, she became the direct ancestor to King David.

A long-standing custom for the feast after the evening meal is to stay awake all night and study. There is a traditional agenda for the study which includes excerpts from many sacred writings of Judaism. A modern addition to the holiday in reform synagogues is Confirmation, a ceremony for fifteen or sixteen year olds, confirming their lifelong commitment to Judaism and Torah study. The feast acknowledges that God gave the Torah long ago, but we are continually in the process of receiving it.

Reflection and discussion

• Why is this festival named Shavuot (Weeks)? What is the significance of the counting of the omer?

• What fruit of my life do I bring to the altar to express my gratitude to God?

• Many Jewish traditions associated with this feast give honor to the Torah. What practices might express my dedication to the word of God in the Scriptures?

Prayer

God of Israel, you entered into covenant with your people at Mount Sinai and gave them the gift of the Torah. Thank you for the teachings and traditions of my ancestors by which they lived as your people. Help me to honor your word with the devotion of my life.

Now there were devout Jews from every nation
under heaven living in Jerusalem.
And at this sound the crowd gathered and was bewildered,
because each one heard them speaking in the native language of each.
Acts 2:5–6

The Coming of God's Spirit at Pentecost

ACTS 2:1–17 ¹*When the day of Pentecost had come, they were all together in one place. ²And suddenly from heaven there came a sound like the rush of a violent wind, and it filled the entire house where they were sitting. ³Divided tongues, as of fire, appeared among them, and a tongue rested on each of them. ⁴All of them were filled with the Holy Spirit and began to speak in other languages, as the Spirit gave them ability.*

⁵Now there were devout Jews from every nation under heaven living in Jerusalem. ⁶And at this sound the crowd gathered and was bewildered, because each one heard them speaking in the native language of each. ⁷Amazed and astonished, they asked, "Are not all these who are speaking Galileans? ⁸And how is it that we hear, each of us, in our own native language? ⁹Parthians, Medes, Elamites, and residents of Mesopotamia, Judea and Cappadocia, Pontus and Asia, ¹⁰Phrygia and Pamphylia, Egypt and the parts of Libya belonging to

Cyrene, and visitors from Rome, both Jews and proselytes, [11]*Cretans and Arabs—in our own languages we hear them speaking about God's deeds of power."* [12]*All were amazed and perplexed, saying to one another, "What does this mean?"* [13]*But others sneered and said, "They are filled with new wine."*

[14]*But Peter, standing with the eleven, raised his voice and addressed them, "Men of Judea and all who live in Jerusalem, let this be known to you, and listen to what I say.* [15]*Indeed, these are not drunk, as you suppose, for it is only nine o'clock in the morning.* [16]*No, this is what was spoken through the prophet Joel:*

[17]*'In the last days it will be, God declares,*

that I will pour out my Spirit upon all flesh,

and your sons and your daughters shall prophesy,

and your young men shall see visions,

and your old men shall dream dreams.'"

During the Second Temple period, including the life of Jesus and the formation of his church, Jewish pilgrims streamed to Jerusalem for the feasts. No matter in what corner of the world Jews lived, Jerusalem and its temple was a holy place where they longed to encounter the presence of God. Thousands of pilgrims poured into the city through every gate and created a noisy tumult. They spoke a variety of languages and were as varied and colorful as the wide world. There were Jews and Jewish converts from Syria and Asia Minor, from Babylonia and Medea, from Cyprus and Greece, and from Egypt and Rome. Side by side were poor Jewish peasants who had traveled from the districts of Palestine on donkeys and rich Jewish merchants who had arrived from distant countries by ship.

Pentecost, meaning "fiftieth," is the Greek designation for the feast of Weeks (Tob 2:1; 2 Macc 12:32). Many elements of Luke's text relate this Pentecost event in Jerusalem to the giving of the Torah to Israel at Mount Sinai. The loud sound and the descending fire (verses 2–3) is reminiscent of God's manifestation on the mountain (Exod 19:16–19). Jewish literature spoke of God's gift of the Torah as divine speech sounding forth from the heavenly fire, a communication from God given in their own language. The gift of God's Spirit to the Jewish disciples of Jesus is parallel to the gift of God's Torah to Israel. God's gift of the Torah to Israel is the primary event at which they became God's people; God's gift of the Spirit is the primary event which formed the disciples of Jesus into his church.

Just as Pentecost is understood in the Jewish tradition to be a completion of Passover, Pentecost is the culmination of the fifty-day season of Easter in the Christian calendar. The fifty-day counting, made with eager anticipation from Passover to Weeks, is paralleled by the Christian anticipation of God's promised Spirit at Pentecost to complete the resurrection event. The gift of God's Spirit is the mature fruit of Christ's resurrection.

According to some Jewish traditions, the counting of the omer was begun on the first Sunday of the Passover festival. The Torah says to make the omer offering (and thus start counting) "the day after the Sabbath" (Lev 23:15). The Sadducees, one of the main sects of Judaism during Second Temple times, believed that Sabbath meant the first Saturday in Passover, and thus the offering was made "the day after the Sabbath," which is Sunday. According to this counting, Jesus was raised from the dead as the first fruits of the barley harvest were being offered in the temple. Paul referred to Christ as the first fruits when referring to his resurrection on the day after the Sabbath: "Christ has been raised from the dead, the first fruits of those who have died" (1 Cor 15:20). Fifty days later, as the Jewish disciples of Jesus had gathered for the feast of Weeks, God gave them the gift of his Holy Spirit. They had waited with eager expectation for the fulfillment of God's promise given through his prophet Joel, "I will pour out my Spirit upon all flesh" (verse 17).

Reflection and discussion

• In what way is God's gift of the Spirit at Pentecost parallel to the gift of the Torah to Israel?

• How does an understanding of the Jewish feast of Weeks enrich my understanding of the Christian feast of Pentecost?

• In what way does Peter interpret the feast of Pentecost as a fulfillment of the words of the prophet Joel?

• How is the gift of the Holy Spirit the completion and fruiton of Easter?

Prayer

God of power and might, you manifested your will through the Torah of Israel and through the gift of the Holy Spirit. Help me to savor each day of my life and to live with eager expectation for the fulfillment of your promises.

You shall live in booths for seven days;
all that are citizens in Israel shall live in booths, so that your generations
may know that I made the people of Israel live in booths when I brought
them out of the land of Egypt. Lev 23:42–43

Keeping the Festival of Tabernacles

LEVITICUS 23:33–44 *³³The Lord spoke to Moses, saying: ³⁴Speak to the people of Israel, saying: On the fifteenth day of this seventh month, and lasting seven days, there shall be the festival of booths to the Lord. ³⁵The first day shall be a holy convocation; you shall not work at your occupations. ³⁶Seven days you shall present the Lord's offerings by fire; on the eighth day you shall observe a holy convocation and present the Lord's offerings by fire; it is a solemn assembly; you shall not work at your occupations.*

³⁷These are the appointed festivals of the Lord, which you shall celebrate as times of holy convocation, for presenting to the Lord offerings by fire—burnt offerings and grain offerings, sacrifices and drink offerings, each on its proper day—³⁸apart from the sabbaths of the Lord, and apart from your gifts, and apart from all your votive offerings, and apart from all your freewill offerings, which you give to the Lord.

³⁹Now, the fifteenth day of the seventh month, when you have gathered in the produce of the land, you shall keep the festival of the Lord, lasting seven days; a complete rest on the first day, and a complete rest on the eighth day. [40] *On the first day you shall take the fruit of majestic trees, branches of palm trees, boughs of leafy trees, and willows of the brook; and you shall rejoice before the Lord your God for seven days.* [41] *You shall keep it as a festival to the Lord seven days in the year; you shall keep it in the seventh month as a statute forever throughout your generations.* [42] *You shall live in booths for seven days; all that are citizens in Israel shall live in booths,* [43] *so that your generations may know that I made the people of Israel live in booths when I brought them out of the land of Egypt: I am the Lord your God.*

[44] *Thus Moses declared to the people of Israel the appointed festivals of the Lord.*

The last of the three great pilgrimage feasts in ancient Israel is called Sukkot in Hebrew. The feast is variously translated as Tabernacles, Booths, Tents, and Huts. It is the fall festival, a joyful feast of thanksgiving. It begins on the full moon of the seventh month (in our September-October).

Like the other pilgrimage festivals, Sukkot was originally an agricultural festival. The most ancient calendars call it the feast of Ingathering (Exod 23:16; 34:22). It marked the ingathering of all the produce of the fruit harvest, especially the olives and the grapes. When the earth had yielded all its fruit for the year, and after it had been gathered and stored, the people gave thanks and worshiped God with sacrifices, singing, and dancing.

The feast gets its name from its most characteristic symbol, the temporary structures in which the Jewish people live during this week each year. The building of the *sukkot* (booths or huts) is rooted in an ancient practice in which the people built improvised shelters in the orchards and vineyards at harvest time. These simple booths offered some protection from the sun during periods of rest. Since the feast of Ingathering was celebrated outdoors where these huts were so much a part of the harvest scene, the festival became known as the feast of Sukkot.

Like the other two pilgrimage feasts, this agricultural festival later became a memorial of Israel's exodus journey. The huts became reminders of the nomadic shelters in which the Israelites lived during their forty years in the wilderness. From age to age, families would spend seven days each year living in temporary huts, as Leviticus says, "so that your generations may know that

I made the people of Israel live in booths when I brought them out of the land of Egypt" (verse 43).

Another ritual aspect of the feast is called the waving of the four species, also called the *lulav* and *etrog*. The Torah commands the Israelites to take four plants and use them in their praise of God during the feast: "You shall take the fruit of majestic trees, branches of palm trees, boughs of leafy trees, and willows of the brook; and you shall rejoice before the Lord your God" (verse 40). The four species, as interpreted by the rabbis of later centuries, are the following: an etrog (a citrus fruit similar to a lemon), a palm branch (in Hebrew, *lulav*), two willow branches (*aravot*) and three myrtle branches (*hadassim*). The six branches are bound and referred to collectively as the lulav, because the palm branch is by far the largest part. The etrog is held in the other hand. The four are all plants native to Israel and represent four types of growing things.

During the days of the temple, the Israelites would form a procession around the temple and wave the four species in praise of God. Today, the four species are held and waved during the Hallel (psalms of praise) and during processions around the *bimah* (the pedestal in the synagogue where the Torah is read) each day during the feast. This part of the service is known as Hoshanot, because while the procession is made, the refrain "Hoshanah!" (Please save us!) is prayed. On the seventh day of Sukkot, seven circuits are made. For this reason, the seventh day of Sukkot is known as Hoshanah Rabbah (the great Hoshanah).

Reflection and discussion

• Why would living in a booth for a week have such a profound effect on children? What lessons in my life, perhaps camping in a tent or dwelling in temporary housing, have taught me similar lessons?

• Why did God want his people to especially remember their time in the wilderness?

• Why do nearly all agricultural societies hold an annual feast after the autumn harvest? What does the feast of Booths teach me about the importance of giving thanks?

• What Christian ritual is similar to the waving of palm branches to shouts of Hosanna? What do the Jewish roots tell me about the meaning of that ritual?

Prayer

Sovereign Lord, all times and seasons belong to you. I praise you for the fruit of the earth and all growing things that sustain our lives on earth. In this temporary life on earth, give me a grateful heart and the ability to surrender all things to you.

Three times a year all your males shall appear before the Lord your God at the place that he will choose: at the festival of unleavened bread, at the festival of weeks, and at the festival of booths. Deut 16:16

Rejoicing at the Feast of Booths

DEUTERONOMY 16:13–17   [13] *You shall keep the festival of booths for seven days, when you have gathered in the produce from your threshing floor and your wine press.* [14] *Rejoice during your festival, you and your sons and your daughters, your male and female slaves, as well as the Levites, the strangers, the orphans, and the widows resident in your towns.* [15] *Seven days you shall keep the festival for the Lord your God at the place that the Lord will choose; for the Lord your God will bless you in all your produce and in all your undertakings, and you shall surely celebrate.*

[16] *Three times a year all your males shall appear before the Lord your God at the place that he will choose: at the festival of unleavened bread, at the festival of weeks, and at the festival of booths. They shall not appear before the Lord empty-handed;* [17] *all shall give as they are able, according to the blessing of the Lord your God that he has given you.*

Before there was a temple in Jerusalem, the Israelites made pilgrimages to sanctuaries in other parts of the land, such as Shiloh (1 Samuel 1:3). But when King Solomon completed the building of the temple, the first feast held there was the celebration of Sukkot. Gradually the focal point for pilgrimage shifted to Jerusalem's temple, and in time the other shrines throughout the land were abolished. Three times a year, the Israelites went up to Jerusalem for the pilgrimage feasts (verse 16). For most of the biblical period, Sukkot was the most crowded and popular of the feasts. In some parts of the Bible it is simply called "the festival."

Every seven years, the Israelites were commanded to gather in Jerusalem during the feast of Booths for a public reading of Deuteronomy, the book that reviews the teachings of the Torah (Deut 31:10–13). The priests blew trumpets to summon everyone, including women and particularly children, who would be influenced by what they heard for the rest of their lives. Surrounded by his people, the king sat on a large platform erected in the temple's court and read aloud. This ceremony, called "the gathering," was a source of spiritual rejuvenation and inspirations for the nation.

The feast of booths is the most unreservedly joyful of all the Jewish festivals. In many writings it is called "the season of our rejoicing." It follows each year on the heals of the Day of Atonement, the most ascetic, self-denying, and sin-conscious of the holy days. The release from the Day of Atonement's somber reflection is followed, four days later, by the outburst of joy and celebration that is Sukkot. On this day, Jews are commanded to eat, drink, dance, and relish life to the fullest while celebrating the harvest and the material blessings of life.

Many religious people assume that fasting and self-denial is more virtuous than feasting and celebrating. But Judaism teaches, especially in the feast of Sukkot, that the appreciation and enjoyment of material goods and worldly pleasures are an essential religious concern. For the Jew, joy is a sacred gift to be relished and treasured. In fact the rabbis taught that, in the world to come, everyone will have to stand in judgment for every legitimate pleasure in this life that they rejected and failed to enjoy (*Jerusalem Talmud*, Kiddushin 4:12). The religious path to God includes enjoying good food, choice wine, nice clothes, loving sexual relations, and joyous moments with family and friends.

Making joy holy means enjoying God's gifts without worshiping or coveting those gifts. Thus, Judaism incorporates the practice of sharing the bounty and joy of ones life with people in need. The text of Deuteronomy commands, "Rejoice during your festival, you and your sons and your daughters, your male and female slaves, as well as the Levites, the strangers, the orphans, and the widows resident in your towns" (verse 14). A special tradition of the feast of Booths is hospitality for honored guests. Every evening a different biblical personality from the past is imaginatively invited to visit the sukkah and join the company. As stand-ins for these biblical figures, families invite people from the local community who are in need of the food and companionship offered within the sukkah.

At the end of the feast of Booths, another festival day is added which concludes the season of rejoicing—Simchat Torah, which means "rejoicing with the Torah." On this day, the community ends its public cycles of Torah readings and begins again. The conclusion of the book of Deuteronomy is proclaimed, and immediately the beginning of the book of Genesis is recited. To celebrate this yearly starting again, the Torah scrolls are removed from the ark (the repository in the synagogue for holding the scrolls) and a festive procession circles the sanctuary seven times, dancing and singing with the Torah scrolls. The circles of the procession mirror the cycle of readings. The image symbolizes the unending, lifelong privilege of Torah learning. Simchat Torah emphasizes the ecstatic delight of studying Torah and the teaching of the rabbis that Jews study Torah their entire lifetime and always find new meaning in it.

Reflection and discussion

• What can Judaism teach me about the importance of celebrating material blessings and earthly pleasures?

• Why does Judaism mandate hospitality to the poor as an important part of rejoicing in life's gifts?

• Why is the rhythm of ascetic fasting followed by joyful feasting so spiritually healthy?

• Why does Judaism celebrate Simchat Torah? What does this feast teach me about the lifelong privilege of studying the Bible?

Prayer

Bountiful God, you are the giver of all good gifts. Thank you for the material blessings and pleasures of my life. Help me to be grateful for all you have given me and to share from my abundance with those in need.

"Go out to the hills and bring branches of olive, wild olive, myrtle,
palm, and other leafy trees to make booths, as it is written."
So the people went out and brought them, and made booths for themselves,
each on the roofs of their houses, and in their courts and in the courts of
the house of God. Neh 8:15–16

Rediscovering the Joys of the Festival

NEHEMIAH 8:13–18 [13]*On the second day the heads of ancestral houses of all the people, with the priests and the Levites, came together to the scribe Ezra in order to study the words of the law.* [14]*And they found it written in the law, which the Lord had commanded by Moses, that the people of Israel should live in booths during the festival of the seventh month,* [15]*and that they should publish and proclaim in all their towns and in Jerusalem as follows, "Go out to the hills and bring branches of olive, wild olive, myrtle, palm, and other leafy trees to make booths, as it is written."* [16]*So the people went out and brought them, and made booths for themselves, each on the roofs of their houses, and in their courts and in the courts of the house of God, and in the square at the Water Gate and in the square at the Gate of Ephraim.* [17]*And all the assembly of those who had returned from the captivity made booths and lived in them; for from the days of Jeshua son of Nun to that day the people of Israel had not done so. And there was* *very great rejoicing.* ¹⁸*And day by day, from the first day to the last day, he read from the book of the law of God. They kept the festival seven days; and on the eighth day there was a solemn assembly, according to the ordinance.*

During the Israelite exile in Babylon (during the sixth century B.C.), the celebration of Sukkot was suspended. Because it was a feast rooted in the land of Israel and its agricultural abundance, there was not much reason to rejoice while in captivity. But when the displaced returned to the land, they enthusiastically renewed the celebration of the festivals, just as they were described while the people studied the Torah with Ezra (verse 13). The renewed Israelites ran out to get olive, myrtle, palm, and other leafy branches for the construction of their temporary shelters (verses 15-16). They made booths in every available space—on the roofs and in the courtyards of their homes, in the courts of the temple, and at the gates of the city. The whole community dwelt in them throughout the city of Jerusalem for the celebration of the festival (verse 17).

A sukkah may be of any size, according to the rabbis, so long as it is large enough to fulfill the commandment of dwelling in it. The roof is the most regulated part and must be put on last. To fulfill the commandment, the roof must be made of material that grew from the ground and was cut off, such a tree branches, vines, corn stalks, bamboo reeds, sticks, or two-by-fours. Its material must be left loose, not tied together or tied down, and placed sparsely so that rain can get in and stars can be seen. The most enjoyable part of the feast's preparation is decorating the sukkah with patterns of fruits, vegetables, flowers, and anything that adds color and life.

In these frail structures, the Jewish people take their meals by candlelight, sing, pray, visit with one another, and sometimes spend the nights during the festival. The moon and stars shine through the loose boughs on the roof, and wind and rain can at any minute make life dreary. At the mercy of nature, the Jewish people live as their ancestors did in the desert for a week out of every year. The charm of camping out each year creates a delightful and memorable experience for instructing the children. In word and symbol, every generation comes to experience themselves as part of the people blessed by God with freedom and life.

Sukkot is a reminder that our true security is not found by dwelling behind the solid walls of our homes. Sometimes the walls we build to protect us serve instead to divide us, cut us off, and lock us in our solitude. The frail sukkah may make people vulnerable to weather, but it also makes them available to people, to offer kindness, to receive support, to hear when another calls, to drop by to see if anyone is up for a coffee and chat. In the little hut, human differences are minimized so that people see their oneness with others and their common humanity. The permeable walls of the sukkah remind us that lasting security is found in openness to God and others, that genuine spirituality is not about what happens behind closed doors, that real freedom is enjoyed by opening our homes and our hearts to one another.

Reflection and discussion

• Why is the material and instructions for the roof of the sukkah so specifically regulated? What are the effects of dwelling in the sukkah?

• In what way is my life confined and isolated? What does the feast of Sukkot teach me about security?

Prayer

God of all people, in my tight security and isolation, let me not forget my deepest needs or those of others. Open my heart to offer simple kindnesses to others, and give me the humility to receive the care of people who reach out to me.

On the last day of the festival, the great day, while Jesus was standing there, he cried out, "Let anyone who is thirsty come to me, and let the one who believes in me drink." John 7:37–38

The Messiah Satisfies the Longings of Israel

JOHN 7:2–10, 14–18, 37–44 ²*Now the Jewish festival of Booths was near. ³So his brothers said to him, "Leave here and go to Judea so that your disciples also may see the works you are doing; ⁴for no one who wants to be widely known acts in secret. If you do these things, show yourself to the world." ⁵(For not even his brothers believed in him.) ⁶Jesus said to them, "My time has not yet come, but your time is always here. ⁷The world cannot hate you, but it hates me because I testify against it that its works are evil. ⁸Go to the festival yourselves. I am not going to this festival, for my time has not yet fully come." ⁹After saying this, he remained in Galilee. ¹⁰But after his brothers had gone to the festival, then he also went, not publicly but as it were in secret.*

¹⁴About the middle of the festival Jesus went up into the temple and began to teach. ¹⁵The Jews were astonished at it, saying, "How does this man have such learning, when he has never been taught?" ¹⁶Then Jesus answered them, "My teaching is not mine but his who sent me. ¹⁷Anyone who resolves to do the will of God will know whether the teaching is from God or whether I am speaking on my own. [18] *Those who speak on their own seek their own glory; but the one who seeks the glory of him who sent him is true, and there is nothing false in him."*

[37] *On the last day of the festival, the great day, while Jesus was standing there, he cried out, "Let anyone who is thirsty come to me,* [38] *and let the one who believes in me drink. As the scripture has said, 'Out of the believer's heart shall flow rivers of living water.'"* [39] *Now he said this about the Spirit, which believers in him were to receive; for as yet there was no Spirit, because Jesus was not yet glorified.*

[40] *When they heard these words, some in the crowd said, "This is really the prophet."* [41] *Others said, "This is the Messiah." But some asked, "Surely the Messiah does not come from Galilee, does he?* [42] *Has not the scripture said that the Messiah is descended from David and comes from Bethlehem, the village where David lived?"* [43] *So there was a division in the crowd because of him.* [44] *Some of them wanted to arrest him, but no one laid hands on him.*

Underlying the feast of Sukkot is its universal and messianic character. Coming at the end of the agricultural year and the end of the pilgrimage cycle, the feast anticipates the end of time and the coming of the Messiah. In those days, as Israel's prophets proclaimed, all the people of the world will go up to Jerusalem to worship God on the feast of Sukkot: "Then all who survive of the nations that have come against Jerusalem shall go up year by year to worship the King, the Lord of hosts, and to keep the festival of booths" (Zech 14:16). This ecumenical vision is reflected in the sukkah, with its door and roof open to all. Further, Jewish literature refers to the temple as God's sukkah, as a house of prayer for all nations. In that future, God will spread a "sukkat shalom," a shelter made of peace and harmony over all.

In the days of Jesus, Sukkot remained a joyful pilgrimage festival. Pilgrims came from throughout the land and from every Jewish community in the world. They came in colorful caravans—traveling by chariot, donkey, camel, and on foot—up to Jerusalem. Once in the city, festive with garlands of olive, palm, and willow branches, and fragrant with flowers, they participated in the colorful religious processions, waving the lulav, singing Hoshanah to God, and feasting in the booths erected in every part of the city. Jesus traveled privately to the feast of Booths because of the confusion and division created by his teaching.

Two aspects of the feast were particularly celebrated at the time of Jesus: the ceremony of light and the water ritual. On every evening of the festival, four immense menorahs (seven-branched candelabra) were set up in the temple's courts. According to rabbinical writings, they generated such intense light that they illuminated every courtyard of the city. An orchestra of flutes, trumpets, harps, and cymbals accompanied torchlight processions, performers dancing and juggling torches, and singing and clapping crowds. On the morning of each day, the temple priests led a ritual called *Simchat Beit Hashoavah* (Rejoicing at the Place of the Water Drawing). The people processed down to the Pool of Siloam to fill a golden flask with water. Trumpet blasts greeted their arrival at the temple's Water Gate, identified by the rabbis as the south gate from which the water of life would flow in the final days (Ezek 47:1–5). Entering the temple, they processed around the altar, as the people waved the lulav and sang the Hallel. Arriving at the altar, the priests poured the water flask together with a flask of wine so that it flowed out over the altar as an offering to God.

The rituals of light and water in the context of Sukkot were powerful symbols, not only of Israel's past, but of the future days of the Messiah. The Coming One, the Jews believed, would bring the definitive gift of water for his thirsting people, just as Moses had brought water from the rock during their exodus journey. The Messiah would also bring light in the night so that the temple would shine brightly, just as the pillar of fire had accompanied God's people through the wilderness (Exod 13:21).

On the final day of the feast, Jesus declared that he is the font of living water, the source of water for all people who thirst for God's Spirit (7:37–39). He also announced, "I am the light of the world. Whoever follows me will never walk in darkness but will have the light of life" (8:12). Within the context of the autumn feast in which the temple became the light of Jerusalem, Jesus declared himself as the fire lighting the way for all people. With these words of Jesus, John's gospel proclaims that he is the fulfillment of the hopes expressed in the rituals of this great feast. Jesus is God's new temple, brightening the whole world with its light, from which flows the water of life for all thirsty pilgrims.

Reflection and discussion

• In what way does the feast of Booths reflect God's universal plan of salvation and prepare for the coming of the Messiah?

• Why is the last day of the feast the ideal time for Jesus to declare himself as the living water and light of the world?

• Jews and Christians both await the same future: the just and peaceful kingdom ruled by God's Messiah. How can we better anticipate God's reign together?

Prayer

God of all people, I long for the day when the whole world will be refreshed with your gift of living water and brightened with eternal light. Deepen my hope in the Messiah's final coming when you will manifest the new Jerusalem and all people will walk by its light.

SUGGESTIONS FOR FACILITATORS, GROUP SESSION 3

1. Welcome group members and ask if there are any announcements anyone would like to make.

2. You may want to pray this prayer as a group:

Lord God of Abraham, Moses, and Jesus, you gave your people the gift of the three pilgrim feasts of Passover, Weeks, and Booths. Give us a deep gratitude for the material blessings you have lavished upon us. Help us to rejoice in the abundance of the gifts we receive on our pilgrimage through life. As you gave your people the Torah and led them through the desert, give us your Spirit and lead us to the abundant life you have promised. As we study these feasts, help us encourage one another with hope and guide us with your Spirit of truth.

3. Ask one or more of the following questions:
   • Which image from the lessons this week stands out most memorably to you?
   • What is the most important lesson you learned through your study this week?

4. Discuss lessons 7 through 12. Choose one or more of the questions for reflection and discussion from each lesson to discuss as a group. You may want to ask group members which question was most challenging or helpful to them as you review each lesson.

5. Remember that there are no definitive answers for these discussion questions. The insights of group members will add to the understanding of all. None of these questions require an expert.

6. After talking about each lesson, instruct group members to complete lessons 13 through 18 on their own during the six days before the next group meeting. They should write out their own answers to the questions as preparation for next week's group discussion.

7. Ask the group if anyone is having any particular problems with the Bible study during the week. You may want to share advice and encouragement within the group.

8. Conclude by praying aloud together the prayer at the end of one of the lessons discussed. You may add to the prayer based on the sharing that has occurred in the group.

In the seventh month, on the first day of the month, you shall observe a day
of complete rest, a holy convocation commemorated with trumpet blasts.
Lev 23:24

Blowing the Trumpets
for Rosh Hashanah

LEVITICUS 23:23–25   ²³ *The Lord spoke to Moses, saying:* ²⁴ *Speak to the
people of Israel, saying: In the seventh month, on the first day of the month, you
shall observe a day of complete rest, a holy convocation commemorated with
trumpet blasts.* ²⁵ *You shall not work at your occupations; and you shall present
the Lord's offering by fire.*

NUMBERS 29:1–6   ¹ *On the first day of the seventh month you shall have a
holy convocation; you shall not work at your occupations. It is a day for you to
blow the trumpets,* ² *and you shall offer a burnt offering, a pleasing odor to the
Lord: one young bull, one ram, seven male lambs a year old without blemish.*
³ *Their grain offering shall be of choice flour mixed with oil, three-tenths of one
ephah for the bull, two-tenths for the ram,* ⁴ *and one-tenth for each of the seven
lambs;* ⁵ *with one male goat for a sin offering, to make atonement for you.* ⁶ *These
are in addition to the burnt offering of the new moon and its grain offering, and*

the regular burnt offering and its grain offering, and their drink offerings, according to the ordinance for them, a pleasing odor, an offering by fire to the Lord.

Rosh Hashanah literally means "head of the year" and is commonly known as the Jewish New Year. The name is deceptive because there are few similarities between Rosh Hashanah and the midnight celebrations, parades, and bowl games that mark January 1 on the secular calendar. The Jewish New Year is a time of introspection, looking back at the mistakes of the past year, and planning for changes in the new year ahead. Rosh Hashanah and the ten days leading to Yom Kippur are profoundly serious days, called "Days of Awe," and totally different in tone from the spirited joy of the other Jewish festivals. Heavily laden with personal probing and responsibility, the Jewish New Year is greeted not with noise and merry-making, but with a solemn and contrite heart.

The seventh month is the most sacred month in the Jewish calendar. It is the month that begins with the sober Days of Awe and continues with the festive feast of Sukkot. In Israel's agricultural days, this month, called Tishri, fell at the critical intersection between the end of the harvest season and the beginning of the rainy season. At this pivotal moment, the Israelites celebrated rituals that renewed their commitment to be good stewards of the world God had entrusted to them. Just as the seventh day of the week is holy, so the seventh month holds special value. The Israelites celebrated the citing of every new moon as a sacred time, so the seventh new moon—counting from Nisan, the first month in the spring—would be particularly holy. The first day of Tishri is commemorated by a day of rest, sacrifices offered, and the sounding of the *shofar*, the ram's horn (Lev 23:24; Num 29:1).

There are at least two new year celebrations in the Jewish calendar: one in the spring month of Nisan, "the first month of the year" (Exod 12:2), and another in the fall at "the turn of the year" (Exod 34:22). This concept doesn't seem so strange when we consider that we mark the beginning of the calendar year, the school year, the liturgical year, and the fiscal year, all in different months. In Judaism, Nissan 1 is the new year for counting the months on the calendar and the annual cycle of feasts. Tishri 1 (Rosh Hashanah) is the new year for counting the years on the Jewish calendar.

Many scholars have suggested that in ancient Israel the first day of the seventh month celebrated the kingship of God over all the earth, a symbolic enthronement of God at the beginning of each new year. There are hints of this celebration in many of the royal psalms which emphasize God as the Creator, King, and Judge (especially Pss 93–100). If the new year enthronement of God was the ancient origin of Rosh Hashanah, then the feast originally celebrated God as the sole creator of the world, who on this day ascended the throne as the ruler and righteous judge over all creation, dispensing justice for the people of the earth—all themes which penetrate the Jewish feast today.

Still today, one of the most important observances of this holiday is hearing the sounding of the shofar in the synagogue. A total of a hundred notes are sounded. Trumpet blasts served a variety of purposes in ancient Israel, including the announcement of the coronation of a king. On this ancient feast, the shofar announced that God is the true king. But the most important purpose for understanding the shofar's use on this feast was the call to Israel to break camp and embark on a mission in response to God's call. The sounding of the shofar stirs God's people to look to the year ahead and to take up the task of living in the world in a way that makes a difference.

Reflection and discussion

• Is the Jewish remembrance of New Year similar or different from the ways I commemorate January 1? What does the Jewish tradition teach me about beginning the year?

• As I read through Psalms 93–100, what do they teach me about honoring God? What seems to be the primary emphasis of these psalms?

• Why does it seem appropriate that the opening days of the new year be called "Days of Awe"?

• In what sense is the sounding of the shofar a rousing call for the Jewish people?

Prayer

Eternal God, you are the source of all our beginnings and the termination of all our endings. Help me to acknowledge you as Creator, King, and Judge. Rule over my life, sustain me in all that I do, and have mercy upon me.

"Go your way, eat the fat and drink sweet wine and send portions of them to those for whom nothing is prepared, for this day is holy to our Lord; and do not be grieved, for the joy of the Lord is your strength." Neh 8:10

Entrusting the New Year to the Lord

NEHEMIAH 8:1–12   ¹*When the seventh month came—the people of Israel being settled in their towns—all the people gathered together into the square before the Water Gate. They told the scribe Ezra to bring the book of the law of Moses, which the Lord had given to Israel. ²Accordingly, the priest Ezra brought the law before the assembly, both men and women and all who could hear with understanding. This was on the first day of the seventh month. ³He read from it facing the square before the Water Gate from early morning until midday, in the presence of the men and the women and those who could understand; and the ears of all the people were attentive to the book of the law. ⁴The scribe Ezra stood on a wooden platform that had been made for the purpose; and beside him stood Mattithiah, Shema, Anaiah, Uriah, Hilkiah, and Maaseiah on his right hand; and Pedaiah, Mishael, Malchijah, Hashum, Hash-baddanah, Zechariah, and Meshullam on his left hand. ⁵And Ezra opened the book in the sight of all the people, for he was standing above all the people; and when he opened it, all the people stood up. ⁶Then Ezra blessed the Lord, the great God, and all the people answered, "Amen, Amen," lift-*

ing up their hands. Then they bowed their heads and worshiped the Lord with their faces to the ground. ⁷Also Jeshua, Bani, Sherebiah, Jamin, Akkub, Shabbethai, Hodiah, Maaseiah, Kelita, Azariah, Jozabad, Hanan, Pelaiah, the Levites, helped the people to understand the law, while the people remained in their places. ⁸So they read from the book, from the law of God, with interpretation. They gave the sense, so that the people understood the reading.

⁹And Nehemiah, who was the governor, and Ezra the priest and scribe, and the Levites who taught the people said to all the people, "This day is holy to the Lord your God; do not mourn or weep." For all the people wept when they heard the words of the law. ¹⁰Then he said to them, "Go your way, eat the fat and drink sweet wine and send portions of them to those for whom nothing is prepared, for this day is holy to our Lord; and do not be grieved, for the joy of the Lord is your strength." ¹¹So the Levites stilled all the people, saying, "Be quiet, for this day is holy; do not be grieved." ¹²And all the people went their way to eat and drink and to send portions and to make great rejoicing, because they had understood the words that were declared to them.

On the first day of the seventh month (verse 2), the people of Israel gathered at the Water Gate of the temple in a dramatic ceremony of covenant renewal. This occurred in the mid-fifth century, B.C., a century or so after their exile in Babylon. Whether the first of Tishri was celebrated at the time as the beginning of the new year is unknown, but the date was certainly the most important of the monthly new moon festivals. Ezra the scribe read from the Torah scrolls to the men, women, and children old enough to understand (verse 3), and the Levites interpreted the text for them, probably translating it from Hebrew to the people's dialect of Aramaic (verse 8). The ceremony was a liturgical proclamation of Scripture, read from a wooden platform above the people. As the scrolls were opened, the people stood up and the reading was preceded by a prayer of blessing (verses 5–6). When the people heard the words of the Torah, they grieved and wept, realizing how much they had neglected the Scriptures and strayed from their teachings (verse 9).

In the following centuries, Rosh Hashana became known as the Day of Judgment. On this day, God is acknowledged as the exalted king and awesome judge, who opens the books of remembrance in which is found the fate of every person. As the great shofar is sounded, all the people of the world pass before God so that their judgment may be inscribed, like sheep pass beneath the staff of the shepherd to be counted and recorded. God watches over the hearts and deeds of his people, as stated in the psalm: "The Lord looks down from heaven; he sees all humankind. From where he sits enthroned he watches all the inhabitants of the earth—he who fashions the hearts of them all, and observes all their deeds"(Ps 33:13–15).

According to this tradition, God opens three books on Rosh Hashanah. In the first, the righteous are inscribed for life in the coming year. In the second, the wicked are inscribed for death. And in the third, the names of those who are not easily classified (which include most people) are temporarily inscribed, while their behavior during the coming Days of Awe culminating on Yom Kippur will decide their fates during the year ahead. A severe decree can be averted during these ten days of repentance. God is described as a merciful judge who understands the frail nature of human beings. The sages teach that three things cancel the decree: prayer, charity, and repentance. The requirements for repentance include a change of mind, a feeling of regret, a determination to change, and an effort to repair the effect of one's misdeeds. Thus, the traditional Jewish greeting of Rosh Hashana: "May you be inscribed and sealed for a good year."

In the synagogue liturgy for Rosh Hashana, the magnificent Unetanah Tokef is recited, a poem describing this yearly day of judgment as "awesome and terrible." God, the eternal king, is contrasted with man, who is "like a broken shard, like dry grass, a withered flower, like a passing shadow and a vanishing cloud, like a breeze that blows away and dust that scatters, like a dream that flies away." Yet the Rosh Hashanah liturgy also stresses that human beings are created by God and have a special relationship with the creator. In dealing with this paradox, the sages offer outstanding advice. They say that each person should carry two notes in his or her pockets. On one would be the words, "For my sake the world was created." On the other, "I am but dust and ashes." When we despair of our value we look at the first. When we are too haughty, we look at the second.

On Rosh Hashana, God's people are called to honestly evaluate themselves in the presence of their just Judge and to take personal responsibility for the quality of their internal hearts and their external deeds. It is a day that is full of hope and good wishes. The *challah* (traditional bread for Sabbath and holidays) and apples are traditionally dipped in honey on this day, symbolizing the hopes for a sweet New Year.

Reflection and discussion

• In what ways does the public reading of the Torah by Ezra have echoes in the liturgical proclamation of the gospels today?

• Do I think of God as the great Judge of the world? In what sense can God's judgment be described as "awesome and terrible"?

• What is the detriment of becoming too haughty or too lowly? In what way does the synagogue liturgy of Rosh Hashanah help people put their lives in perspective?

Prayer

Just and merciful Judge, you watch over the quality of our hearts and our deeds. Though I am but dust and ashes, you have made me to live with you for eternity. Humble me before your majesty and give me hope in the glorious destiny you plan for me.

He shall slaughter the goat of the sin offering that is for the people
and bring its blood inside the curtain, and do with its blood as he did
with the blood of the bull, sprinkling it upon the mercy seat
and before the mercy seat. Lev 16:15

Sacrifices for the Day of Atonement

LEVITICUS 16:2–19 ²*The Lord said to Moses: Tell your brother Aaron not to come just at any time into the sanctuary inside the curtain before the mercy seat that is upon the ark, or he will die; for I appear in the cloud upon the mercy seat. ³Thus shall Aaron come into the holy place: with a young bull for a sin offering and a ram for a burnt offering. ⁴He shall put on the holy linen tunic, and shall have the linen undergarments next to his body, fasten the linen sash, and wear the linen turban; these are the holy vestments. He shall bathe his body in water, and then put them on. ⁵He shall take from the congregation of the people of Israel two male goats for a sin offering, and one ram for a burnt offering.*

⁶Aaron shall offer the bull as a sin offering for himself, and shall make atonement for himself and for his house. ⁷He shall take the two goats and set them before the Lord at the entrance of the tent of meeting; ⁸and Aaron shall cast lots on the two goats, one lot for the Lord and the other lot for Azazel. ⁹Aaron shall present the goat on which the lot fell for the Lord, and offer it as a sin offering; ¹⁰but the goat on which the lot fell for Azazel shall be presented alive before the Lord to make atonement over it, that it may be sent away into the wilderness to Azazel.

¹¹*Aaron shall present the bull as a sin offering for himself, and shall make atonement for himself and for his house; he shall slaughter the bull as a sin offering for himself.* ¹²*He shall take a censer full of coals of fire from the altar before the Lord, and two handfuls of crushed sweet incense, and he shall bring it inside the curtain* ¹³*and put the incense on the fire before the Lord, that the cloud of the incense may cover the mercy seat that is upon the covenant, or he will die.* ¹⁴*He shall take some of the blood of the bull, and sprinkle it with his finger on the front of the mercy seat, and before the mercy seat he shall sprinkle the blood with his finger seven times.*

¹⁵*He shall slaughter the goat of the sin offering that is for the people and bring its blood inside the curtain, and do with its blood as he did with the blood of the bull, sprinkling it upon the mercy seat and before the mercy seat.* ¹⁶*Thus he shall make atonement for the sanctuary, because of the uncleannesses of the people of Israel, and because of their transgressions, all their sins; and so he shall do for the tent of meeting, which remains with them in the midst of their uncleannesses.* ¹⁷*No one shall be in the tent of meeting from the time he enters to make atonement in the sanctuary until he comes out and has made atonement for himself and for his house and for all the assembly of Israel.* ¹⁸*Then he shall go out to the altar that is before the Lord and make atonement on its behalf, and shall take some of the blood of the bull and of the blood of the goat, and put it on each of the horns of the altar.* ¹⁹*He shall sprinkle some of the blood on it with his finger seven times, and cleanse it and hallow it from the uncleannesses of the people of Israel.*

In the days of the temple, Yom Kippur, the Day of Atonement, was the holiest day of the year and often called "The Great Day." All Jews would turn their hearts that day to the temple, where the high priest would conduct the sacred ceremonies. Still today, the Jewish people consider Yom Kippur as the most solemn day of the year. The observances of Rosh Hashana and Yom Kippur comprise the High Holy Days, and the period that encompasses these two days is called in the Talmud, the Ten Days of Repentance.

The depiction of the ancient Day of Atonement in the book of Leviticus is read in the synagogue. The description forms the pivotal center of the book, and thereby the center of the Torah's five books. The account takes us back to the wilderness of the exodus and the ritual performed in the desert sanctuary by Aaron, the priest and brother of Moses. This ritual prefigured the ceremonies in the temple of Jerusalem performed by the high priests in later centuries. The Day of Atonement was the annual rite in which the high priest was empowered to cleanse both the temple and the people from the sin that diminished their witness and compromised God's presence. The elaborate ceremonies offered the promise of God's forgiveness, another chance to live as stewards of God's image in the world, to fulfill the keynote command of God in Leviticus: "You shall be holy, for I the Lord your God am holy" (19:2).

The high priest could pass beyond the curtain of the sanctuary and enter the Holy of Holies only on this one day of the year. Because entering the presence of God was such a dangerous venture, Aaron and the high priests who followed him were required to prepare and follow a prescribed ritual of preparation lest they should die during the encounter (verse 2). After taking purification baths, the high priest laid aside the ornate garments of his office and clothed himself in white linen garments (verse 4) as an expression of the humility and penitential spirit necessary to perform his sacred duties.

After sacrificing a bull for his own sin offering and a goat for that of the people, the high priest entered into the Holy of Holies to officiate in the presence of God. He brought a censer full of fiery coals and finely ground incense. The smoke from the incense upon the coals obscured the divine presence so that God's majestic holiness would be bearable by a sinful man (verses 12–13). He then sprinkled the sacrificial blood, first of the bull and then of the goat, upon the "mercy seat" which covered the Ark of the Covenant in order to atone for his own sins and for the sins of the people (verses 14–15). Since blood is the essence of life (Lev 17:11), the shedding of blood in sacrifice symbolizes a life laid down on behalf of others, and the sprinkling of the blood applies the effects of the sacrifice, bringing cleansing and forgiveness.

Reflection and discussion

• In what way does sin diminish the effectiveness of people, sacred places, and institutions?

• Why is the offering of sacrificial blood such a common practice in ancient cultures for atonement for sins?

• Why was the Day of Atonement so significant for ancient Israel? Why are rituals of reconciliation important for me?

• How does the Jewish tradition teach me that repentance must be experienced inwardly and expressed outwardly?

Prayer

God of mercy, you are majestic in holiness and generous in forgiveness. Cleanse and forgive me of my sin and the sins of your people so that we may always reflect your image in the world. Help me to be holy as you are holy.

This shall be an everlasting statute for you, to make atonement for the people of Israel once in the year for all their sins. Lev 16:34

Annual Rituals for Yom Kippur

LEVITICUS 16:20–34 ²⁰ *When he has finished atoning for the holy place and the tent of meeting and the altar, he shall present the live goat.* ²¹ *Then Aaron shall lay both his hands on the head of the live goat, and confess over it all the iniquities of the people of Israel, and all their transgressions, all their sins, putting them on the head of the goat, and sending it away into the wilderness by means of someone designated for the task.* ²² *The goat shall bear on itself all their iniquities to a barren region; and the goat shall be set free in the wilderness.*

²³ *Then Aaron shall enter the tent of meeting, and shall take off the linen vestments that he put on when he went into the holy place, and shall leave them there.* ²⁴ *He shall bathe his body in water in a holy place, and put on his vestments; then he shall come out and offer his burnt offering and the burnt offering of the people, making atonement for himself and for the people.* ²⁵ *The fat of the sin offering he shall turn into smoke on the altar.* ²⁶ *The one who sets the goat free for Azazel shall wash his clothes and bathe his body in water, and afterward may come into the camp.* ²⁷ *The bull of the sin offering and the goat of the sin offering, whose blood was brought in to make atonement in the holy place, shall be taken*

*outside the camp; their skin and their flesh and their dung shall be consumed in fire. *[28]*The one who burns them shall wash his clothes and bathe his body in water, and afterward may come into the camp.*

*[29]*This shall be a statute to you forever: In the seventh month, on the tenth day of the month, you shall deny yourselves, and shall do no work, neither the citizen nor the alien who resides among you. *[30]*For on this day atonement shall be made for you, to cleanse you; from all your sins you shall be clean before the Lord. *[31]*It is a sabbath of complete rest to you, and you shall deny yourselves; it is a statute forever. *[32]*The priest who is anointed and consecrated as priest in his father's place shall make atonement, wearing the linen vestments, the holy vestments. *[33]*He shall make atonement for the sanctuary, and he shall make atonement for the tent of meeting and for the altar, and he shall make atonement for the priests and for all the people of the assembly. *[34]*This shall be an everlasting statute for you, to make atonement for the people of Israel once in the year for all their sins. And Moses did as the Lord had commanded him.*

The rituals for the elimination of sin and impurity in ancient Israel reached their culmination on the Day of Atonement. The purification processes—sprinkling sacrificial blood in the sanctuary and the ritual of the scapegoat—removed human transgression against the holiness of God, beginning in the temple's inner sanctuary and extending to the farthest fringes of the inhabited land.

The rituals of atonement for the sins of the people were performed with two goats. One was sacrificed as a sin offering to God; the other was designated as the scapegoat, to be sent away to Azazel, the demon of the harsh wilderness (verses 7–10). The high priest placed both hands on the live goat's head, confessing all the sins of Israel over it, and sent it away into the desert (verses 20–22). The people's sins were thus removed as far away as possible and done away with. Sin does not belong with God's covenanted people, so it is taken back to its source among the wild spirits of the wilderness.

The annual Day of Atonement, originally a ritual performed by the high priest alone, increasingly became a public day of repentance. In the days of the Second Temple, the services became more elaborate and involved all the people. The nation became more aware that sin drove out the Holy Presence, both from the temple and from within the individual. People became more aware of their need to attain forgiveness and atonement for their own sins as well as the sins of the nation. It became customary for everyone to spend the entire day in fasting and prayer.

With the destruction of the temple, the Yom Kippur rituals associated with the temple and its priesthood could no longer be performed. As rabbinical Judaism developed, atonement rituals increasingly focused on the synagogue and the individual. A story of two rabbis illustrates the development: "They beheld the temple ruins. 'Woe is us!' cried Rabbi Joshua, 'that the place where the iniquities of Israel were atoned for is now laid waste!' 'My son,' replied Rabbi Yohanan, 'do not be grieved. We have another atonement as effective as this. And what is it? Acts of loving-kindness.'"

The Ten Days of Repentance, from Rosh Hashana to Yom Kippur, are a period of repentance, a process of turning away from selfish ways and turning toward God and other people, and most important, turning toward the true self. God's judgment, which began on Rosh Hashana, is completed and the verdict issued on Yom Kippur. Many Jews view Yom Kippur as a brush with death, a reflection upon mortality. For that reason, they wear a white *kittel*, a robe that will one day serve as their shroud. They abstain from the daily physical activities that keep them alive—eating and drinking. It becomes a day to confront the mortality that we spend most of our lives denying. Like any face-to-face confrontation with death, it can awaken us to live more fully and faithfully.

Reflection and discussion

• What was the meaning of the ritual of the scapegoat in the days of Israel's temple?

• In what way do I experience the withdrawal of God's presence in the face of sin? Does God truly leave, or does it feel like God withdraws from my perspective?

• How have reminders of mortality and confrontations with death encouraged me to live my life more fully?

• How can one day of fasting, prayer, and loving deeds gradually transform every day of my life?

Prayer

God of our ancestors, your presence which dwelt within Israel's temple also fills the temple of my body. Help me to repent of my sins, of all that is contrary to my truest self. May the words and actions of my life radiate your presence to the world.

It is a day of atonement, to make atonement
on your behalf before the Lord your God.
For anyone who does not practice self-denial during that
entire day shall be cut off from the people. Lev 23:28–29

A Day of Fasting and Repentance

LEVITICUS 23:26–32 ²⁶*The Lord spoke to Moses, saying:* ²⁷*Now, the tenth day of this seventh month is the day of atonement; it shall be a holy convocation for you: you shall deny yourselves and present the Lord's offering by fire;* ²⁸*and you shall do no work during that entire day; for it is a day of atonement, to make atonement on your behalf before the Lord your God.* ²⁹*For anyone who does not practice self-denial during that entire day shall be cut off from the people.* ³⁰*And anyone who does any work during that entire day, such a one I will destroy from the midst of the people.* ³¹*You shall do no work: it is a statute forever throughout your generations in all your settlements.* ³²*It shall be to you a sabbath of complete rest, and you shall deny yourselves; on the ninth day of the month at evening, from evening to evening you shall keep your sabbath.*

Yom Kippur, the tenth day of the seventh month, is a Sabbath-like day on which no work may be done, a day characterized by the practice of self-denial. This denial of self, literally "afflicting one's soul," is first and foremost identified as fasting, but the rabbis added prohibitions against washing, anointing with oil, wearing leather shoes, and having sexual relations. These are all proscriptions associated with Jewish mourning practices, for the Day of Atonement is considered a day of grief and mourning.

The day is primarily known as a day of full twenty-four-hour fasting. Most Jews in good health abstain on Yom Kippur from eating or drinking anything. This day of intense self-searching and earnest communication with the Almighty is facilitated by the inner awareness and calm brought on by fasting. The self-assessment required on this day necessitates self-discipline, and fasting demonstrates a willingness to submit to the discipline necessary for progress in the spiritual life. The self-disciple required for the very private matter of curbing our appetite helps individuals commit to the more difficult discipline required for a life of loving deeds toward others and a life of public justice.

The prophetic reading from the synagogue service of Yom Kipper expresses the ultimate goal of fasting: "Is this not the fast that I choose: to loose the bonds of injustice, to undo the thongs of the yoke, to let the oppressed go free, and to break every yoke? Is it not to share your bread with the hungry, and bring the homeless poor into your house; when you see the naked to cover them, and not to hide yourself from your own kin?" (Isa 58:6–7). Atonement demands more than twenty-four hours of abstinence from food. It demands that upon the completion of our fast we will turn back to the world prepared to act with compassion and justice.

Fasting is a traditional practice in nearly every ancient culture and world religion. While our modern society has become increasingly self-indulgent, fasting brings us in the opposite direction. Though our contemporary culture desires happiness beyond all else, fasting helps us understand that some amount of suffering can be beneficial. The satisfaction one can obtain from the self-induced pain of fasting offers insight into a better way of responding to life's inevitable suffering. In the face of a society that constantly bombards us with advertising telling us that we must have this and that to be happy and fulfilled, fasting asserts that we do not need to be dependent on external things for our truest welfare. If we can suspend our most basic need for food and drink for twenty-four hours, how much more can we ignore our craving for all the non-essentials?

Judaism doesn't advocate asceticism for its own sake. In fact, it is contrary to Jewish law to deny one's self the normal pleasures of life. But in our overheated consumer society, it is important to periodically turn off the pressure to consume and to remind ourselves of life's essentials. The self-denial of the Day of Atonement must always lead to transformation of life, to deeper wisdom, compassion, and purpose. In the end, the prayers and self-denial of Yom Kippur express a modest request of God: to give his people but one more year to try again, to live in such a way as to make a difference.

Reflection and discussion

• Why is fasting an important practice in nearly every ancient religion? What are some of the primary benefits of fasting?

• In what way have I found the practice of self-denial to be a positive means of personal change?

• Why did the rabbis choose Isaiah 58 as the text from the prophets to be read on Yom Kippur? What new perspective on fasting does it offer me?

• How do practices of self-denial offer me an alternative perspective to the lures of consumer advertising?

• What wisdom did Christianity learn from the ancient practices of Yom Kippur?

Prayer

Lord God, in the midst of all of life's abundant blessings you call your people to self-denial. May my prayer, fasting, and charity come from a heart transformed by your mercy. Give me a spirit of discipline, compassion, and justice as I seek to make a difference in the world.

Christ entered once for all into the Holy Place, not with the blood of goats and calves, but with his own blood, thus obtaining eternal redemption. Heb 9:12

Atonement through Eternal Redemption

HEBREWS 9:6–14 *⁶Such preparations having been made, the priests go continually into the first tent to carry out their ritual duties; ⁷but only the high priest goes into the second, and he but once a year, and not without taking the blood that he offers for himself and for the sins committed unintentionally by the people. ⁸By this the Holy Spirit indicates that the way into the sanctuary has not yet been disclosed as long as the first tent is still standing. ⁹This is a symbol of the present time, during which gifts and sacrifices are offered that cannot perfect the conscience of the worshiper, ¹⁰but deal only with food and drink and various baptisms, regulations for the body imposed until the time comes to set things right.*

¹¹But when Christ came as a high priest of the good things that have come, then through the greater and perfect tent (not made with hands, that is, not of this creation), ¹²he entered once for all into the Holy Place, not with the blood of goats and calves, but with his own blood, thus obtaining eternal redemption. ¹³For if the blood of goats and bulls, with the sprinkling of the ashes of a heifer, sanctifies those who have been defiled so that their flesh is purified, ¹⁴how much more will the blood of Christ, who through the eternal Spirit offered himself without blemish to God, purify our conscience from dead works to worship the living God!

The destruction of Jerusalem's temple, in A.D. 70, created a crisis for the future of Israel's ancient traditions. With the temple in ruins and its priesthood and system of sacrifices shattered, the ancient faith had to find a new expression of its ancient truth. Both rabbinical Judaism and apostolic Christianity arose to carry on the divine revelation expressed in the Old Testament Scriptures. In their earliest days, the Jews of the synagogue and the Jews who believed in Jesus as the Messiah were closely joined in faith and practice. The Jews who followed Jesus after his death and resurrection continued to see themselves as united to the rich Jewish tradition that formed the faith of the Redeemer. To the degree that Christianity separated itself from its roots in the faith of ancient Israel and defined itself in contrast to Judaism, faith in Jesus was impoverished. As Rabbi Abraham Heschel has written, "A Christian ought to realize that a world without Israel will be a world without Israel's God."

The temple rituals of Yom Kippur express a deeply felt need within all people. We want access to the inner sanctuary, to have a direct experience of the living God and his merciful forgiveness. We all long for a fresh start, freedom from guilt, a healed spirit. We need what was expressed by the high priest in the Holy of Holies through the Day of Atonement's annual ritual.

The letter to the Hebrews proclaims that the atonement accomplished for ancient Israel now happens in the spaciousness of the cosmos for all of humanity. Jesus Christ is both the high priest and the perfect sacrifice offered for sins. The blood of bulls and goats is replaced by the blood of Christ, and thereby, the redemption offered to humanity is eternal (verse 12). The once-a-year entry of the high priest into the Holy Place is fulfilled in the once-for-all sacrifice of Christ.

The earliest Christians were able to understand God's revelation in Christ only through the ancient Scriptures and feasts of Israel. Today's Christians can understand the crucial significance of Good Friday and the sacrificial nature of the Eucharist only through an understanding of what God revealed in the Jewish feast of Yom Kippur. In laying down the revelations of Leviticus concerning the Day of Atonement, the Torah teaches: "This shall be a statute to you forever" (Lev 16:29). The eternal truths of God are rooted in the faith of Israel. When we separate ourselves from our elder brothers and sisters in Judaism, we impoverish God's revelation. When we approach the all-holy God, we come as a people whose pilgrim way has been prepared by the abiding ministries of both Aaron and Jesus.

Reflection and discussion

• In what ways does the sacrifice of Christ complete the rituals of Israel's Day of Atonement?

• In what sense might the Day of Atonement be considered by Christians as an eternal statute given to us by God?

• In what ways do I see Judaism as enriching my Christian beliefs and practices?

Prayer

God of All, peoples and nations long to encounter your all-holy presence and experience your merciful forgiveness. Give me a deep respect for the traditions of my ancestors in faith, and help me to understand the truths of your ancient covenant.

SUGGESTIONS FOR FACILITATORS, GROUP SESSION 4

1. Welcome group members and ask if anyone has any questions, announcements, or requests.

2. You may want to pray this prayer as a group:

Creator, King, and Judge, you rule over our lives and sustain us in all that we do. You are forever offering your people new beginnings so that we can repent of the mistakes of the past and entrust our lives to you. As we study the feasts of the New Year and the Day of Atonement, help us to understand the annual cycles of renewal and grace offered to the people of the covenant. Give us a spirit of repentance as we discover the rich heritage of these Days of Awe. Through fasting, self-denial, and almsgiving, give us the gift of discipline, justice, and compassion. May we always be found in your Book of Life, showing forth your image of holiness and mercy to the world.

3. Ask one or more of the following questions:
   • What is the most difficult part of this study for you?
   • What insight stands out to you from the lessons this week?

4. Discuss lessons 13 through 18. Choose one or more of the questions for reflection and discussion from each lesson to discuss as a group. You may want to ask group members which question was most challenging or helpful to them as you review each lesson.

5. Keep the discussion moving, but allow time for the questions that provoke the most discussion. Encourage the group members to use "I" language in their responses.

6. After talking over each lesson, instruct group members to complete lessons 19 through 24 on their own during the six days before the next group meeting. They should write out their own answers to the questions as preparation for next week's session.

7. Ask the group what encouragement they need for the coming week. Ask the members to pray for the needs of one another during the week.

8. Conclude by praying aloud together the prayer at the end of one of the lessons discussed. You may choose to conclude the prayer by asking members to pray aloud any requests they may have.

He burned the house of the Lord, the king's house,
and all the houses of Jerusalem;
every great house he burned down. 2 Kings 25:9

Lamentations on the Ninth of Av

LAMENTATIONS 1:1–11

¹*How lonely sits the city*
  that once was full of people!
How like a widow she has become,
  she that was great among the nations!
She that was a princess among the provinces
  has become a vassal.

²*She weeps bitterly in the night,*
  with tears on her cheeks;
among all her lovers
  she has no one to comfort her;
all her friends have dealt treacherously with her,
  they have become her enemies.

³*Judah has gone into exile with suffering*
  and hard servitude;
she lives now among the nations,
  and finds no resting place;
her pursuers have all overtaken her
  in the midst of her distress.

⁴*The roads to Zion mourn,*
  for no one comes to the festivals;
all her gates are desolate,
  her priests groan;
her young girls grieve,
  and her lot is bitter.

⁵*Her foes have become the masters,*
  her enemies prosper,
because the Lord has made her suffer
  for the multitude of her transgressions;
her children have gone away,
  captives before the foe.

⁶*From daughter Zion has departed*
  all her majesty.
Her princes have become like stags
  that find no pasture;
they fled without strength
  before the pursuer.

⁷*Jerusalem remembers,*
  in the days of her affliction and wandering,
all the precious things
  that were hers in days of old.
When her people fell into the hand of the foe,
  and there was no one to help her,
the foe looked on mocking
  over her downfall.

[8]*Jerusalem sinned grievously,*
  so she has become a mockery;
all who honored her despise her,
  for they have seen her nakedness;
she herself groans,
  and turns her face away.

[9]*Her uncleanness was in her skirts;*
  she took no thought of her future;
her downfall was appalling,
  with none to comfort her.
"O Lord, look at my affliction,
  for the enemy has triumphed!"

[10]*Enemies have stretched out their hands*
  over all her precious things;
she has even seen the nations
  invade her sanctuary,
those whom you forbade
  to enter your congregation.

[11]*All her people groan*
  as they search for bread;
they trade their treasures for food
  to revive their strength.
Look, O Lord, and see
  how worthless I have become.

Tisha B'Av, the ninth day of the Jewish month of Av (in our July-August), is a day of communal mourning. It commemorates the destruction of Jerusalem and the temple, first by the Babylonians and then again by the Romans. The day is governed by the traditional Jewish mourning code: abstinence from eating, drinking, washing, sexual intimacy, wearing leather shoes, and other pleasurable and extraneous activities. At the last meal before sundown before the fast begins, it is customary to eat an egg sprinkled with ashes. The egg evokes the cycle of life, and the ashes, of course, call to mind the loss and destruction of the day. Many people visit cemeteries on this day, in addition to participating in mournful prayer in the synagogue.

The tone of the synagogue services is created with dimmed light and candles. The ornamental curtain which usually covers the ark (the container for the scrolls of the Scripture) is removed and the decorative pulpit cover is taken away. The congregation assembles in the darkened synagogue, talking in the hushed tones of bereavement. There are no greetings, no laughter; the people sit on low stools, with heads bowed in mourning. The book of Lamentations is chanted using special musical notations that create a tone of weeping, followed by several *kinot* (dirges and other poems of lamentation written at various times of tragedy and destruction).

The book of Lamentations was written out of the ashes and ruins of the first destruction of Jerusalem. The opening words (translated "How!") is actually a primal yell (in Hebrew "Eikhaaah!"), the kind of expression to which language is often reduced by extreme anguish. The lament opens ominously at night (verse 2), and is written in the mournful cadence of a funeral dirge. The tone is sad and somber, matching the eerie darkness. The fractured images of Jerusalem's intense suffering are expressed through the image of the city personified as a woman. We are confronted with the unbearable pain of the ravaged, abandoned, uncomforted daughter Zion. She is a woman exiled and homeless, a refugee relentlessly pursued by her captors (verse 3); she is a mother forced to watch her children taken into captivity (verse 5); she is a woman subjected to sexual assault and rape (verses 8–10). Both the people and the architecture express total suffering: the roads mourn; the gates are deserted; the priests groan; the maidens grieve (verse 4).

In the darkened synagogue, the book is chanted softly at first. Several readers often take turns with different sections of the dirge. Then the readers' voices build to the climax, which is sung aloud by the entire congregation: "Restore us to yourself, O Lord, that we may be restored; renew our days as of old" (Lam 5:21). Following the reading, the rabbi often leads a discussion related to the themes of tragedy and loss.

In Jerusalem, the day is often observed at the Kotel, the Western Wall. This is the only remaining part of the temple foundation. Though the temple has not been standing for close to two millennia, its memory is still a vital part of the collective memory of Judaism. The pilgrimage feasts and sacrifices of old remain as hopeful images of the messianic age to come.

Reflection and discussion

• In what ways is a tone of mourning created in the synagogue services of Tisha B'Av?

• Why do people commemorate painful experiences from the past? In what ways do I express communal grief?

• Which phrase of Lamentations expresses an emotion I have felt in the past?

Prayer

Faithful God, you allow your people to be afflicted with suffering and grief, yet you offer the comforting hope of your merciful presence. Do not forget your afflicted people or ignore the cries of your suffering children. Give me confidence in your faithfulness and trust in your promises.

These days should be remembered and kept throughout every generation, in every family, province, and city; and these days of Purim should never fall into disuse among the Jews, nor should the commemoration of these days cease among their descendants. Esth 9:28

Joy and Feasting at Purim

ESTHER 9:18–32 ¹⁸ *But the Jews who were in Susa gathered on the thirteenth day and on the fourteenth, and rested on the fifteenth day, making that a day of feasting and gladness.* ¹⁹ *Therefore the Jews of the villages, who live in the open towns, hold the fourteenth day of the month of Adar as a day for gladness and feasting, a holiday on which they send gifts of food to one another.*

²⁰ *Mordecai recorded these things, and sent letters to all the Jews who were in all the provinces of King Ahasuerus, both near and far,* ²¹ *enjoining them that they should keep the fourteenth day of the month Adar and also the fifteenth day of the same month, year by year,* ²² *as the days on which the Jews gained relief from their enemies, and as the month that had been turned for them from sorrow into gladness and from mourning into a holiday; that they should make them days of feasting and gladness, days for sending gifts of food to one another and presents to the poor.* ²³ *So the Jews adopted as a custom what they had begun to do, as Mordecai had written to them.*

²⁴ *Haman son of Hammedatha the Agagite, the enemy of all the Jews, had plotted against the Jews to destroy them, and had cast Pur—that is "the lot"—to*

crush and destroy them; [25]*but when Esther came before the king, he gave orders in writing that the wicked plot that he had devised against the Jews should come upon his own head, and that he and his sons should be hanged on the gallows.* [26]*Therefore these days are called Purim, from the word Pur. Thus because of all that was written in this letter, and of what they had faced in this matter, and of what had happened to them,* [27]*the Jews established and accepted as a custom for themselves and their descendants and all who joined them, that without fail they would continue to observe these two days every year, as it was written and at the time appointed.* [28]*These days should be remembered and kept throughout every generation, in every family, province, and city; and these days of Purim should never fall into disuse among the Jews, nor should the commemoration of these days cease among their descendants.*

[29]*Queen Esther daughter of Abihail, along with the Jew Mordecai, gave full written authority, confirming this second letter about Purim.* [30]*Letters were sent wishing peace and security to all the Jews, to the one hundred twenty-seven provinces of the kingdom of Ahasuerus,* [31]*and giving orders that these days of Purim should be observed at their appointed seasons, as the Jew Mordecai and Queen Esther enjoined on the Jews, just as they had laid down for themselves and for their descendants regulations concerning their fasts and their lamentations.* [32]*The command of Queen Esther fixed these practices of Purim, and it was recorded in writing.*

The feast of Purim is celebrated on the fourteenth day of Adar (in our February-March). The festival originated outside the land of Israel, probably among the Jews living in Persia, and commemorates the escape of the Jewish community from a planned genocide. The feast is based on the book of Esther, the story of how Esther, a Jewish queen, and her cousin Mordecai saved their people from the evil plot of the king's advisor, Haman. The word *purim* means "lots" and refers to the casting of lots used by Haman to determine the day of the Jewish extermination (verses 24–26).

Purim is the festival of Jewish deliverance. The story in the book of Esther could be described as a Jewish novel, similar to the books of Ruth, Jonah, Judith, and Tobit. Set in the context of ancient days, the characters express realities that the Jewish people experience over and over, even to this very day. It is no coincidence that the names Mordecai and Esther resemble the

Babylonian deities, Marduk and Ishtar, since mythological themes are woven throughout the saga. The Esther romance is based on the motif of the woman who, through her beauty, captures the heart of the enemy and saves her people from catastrophe, a story similar to the book of Judith.

Wherever the Jews lived, new Hamans arose to persecute them. The book of Esther is a story of the Jewish lot among the nations of the world. Haman's report to the king is a typical statement of anti-Semitism: "There is a certain people scattered and separated among the peoples in all the provinces of your kingdom; their laws are different from those of every other people, and they do not keep the king's laws, so it is not appropriate for the king to tolerate them" (3:8). This type of reasoning has, again and again throughout Jewish history, been the rationale for the persecution of the Jews. But it is the hope that the book gives to the oppressed and scattered Jews everywhere that makes it so beloved. The celebration of Purim assures the Jewish people that, no matter how desperate their circumstances, they will prevail.

The feast of Purim depicts a world turned upside down—in which a Jewish orphan becomes a Persian queen, the architect of a plot to kill the Jews dies at the hands of his target, and a persecuted community institutes a joyful holiday for Jews everywhere. This upside-down-ness is celebrated in a variety of ways during Purim. Both adults and children wear costumes and masks, making merry in carnival style. Noise-making and revelry, even in the synagogue, is acceptable on this day. The usual limitations on drinking are suspended, and the rabbis taught that on Purim one could drink until he could no longer distinguish between "Cursed be Haman!" and "Blessed be Mordecai!" The usual standards of propriety are waved while sharp wit and jest become the order of the day. In this way, Purim has given rise to a rich literature of Jewish satire and parody. It is a day in which rules and boundaries are deliberately blurred, a kind of safety value which lets loose in revelry all the pent up pressures of the year. By inviting people to relinquish their normal modes of behavior for a day, the feast provides a healthy outlet for questioning and challenging the religious system as a preparation for living more authentically within it.

Reflection and discussion

• In what way is the book of Esther the story of what the Jewish people experience over and over again? How does the attitude expressed by the report of Haman (3:8) breed bigotry and persecution?

• The feast of Purim is totally light-hearted and playful. Why do people need days like this?

• How can it be considered healthy to question and challenge one's own religious system?

Prayer

Lord God, you turn our sorrow into gladness and our mourning into joy. Thank you for turning my expectations upside-down and offering me reversals and surprises. Deliver me from the constancy of oppressive seriousness and always-solemn endeavor.

The king rose from the feast in wrath and went into the palace garden, but Haman stayed to beg his life from Queen Esther, for he saw that the king had determined to destroy him. Esth 7:7

Queen Esther Saves Her People

ESTHER 7:1–10 ¹*So the king and Haman went in to feast with Queen Esther. *²On the second day, as they were drinking wine, the king again said to Esther, "What is your petition, Queen Esther? It shall be granted you. And what is your request? Even to the half of my kingdom, it shall be fulfilled." *³Then Queen Esther answered, "If I have won your favor, O king, and if it pleases the king, let my life be given me—that is my petition—and the lives of my people— that is my request. *⁴For we have been sold, I and my people, to be destroyed, to be killed, and to be annihilated. If we had been sold merely as slaves, men and women, I would have held my peace; but no enemy can compensate for this dam- age to the king." *⁵Then King Ahasuerus said to Queen Esther, "Who is he, and where is he, who has presumed to do this?" *⁶Esther said, "A foe and enemy, this wicked Haman!" Then Haman was terrified before the king and the queen.

*⁷The king rose from the feast in wrath and went into the palace garden, but Haman stayed to beg his life from Queen Esther, for he saw that the king had determined to destroy him. *⁸When the king returned from the palace garden to* *the banquet hall, Haman had thrown himself on the couch where Esther was reclining; and the king said, "Will he even assault the queen in my presence, in my own house?" As the words left the mouth of the king, they covered Haman's face. ⁹Then Harbona, one of the eunuchs in attendance on the king, said, "Look, the very gallows that Haman has prepared for Mordecai, whose word saved the king, stands at Haman's house, fifty cubits high." And the king said, "Hang him on that." ¹⁰So they hanged Haman on the gallows that he had prepared for Mordecai. Then the anger of the king abated.*

The feast of Purim carries with it four obligations: to listen to the reading of the book of Esther, to make a joyful feast, to send gifts of food to neighbors and friends, and to be extra generous to the poor. Before the feasting, merrymaking, and gift-giving begins, the scroll of Esther is unrolled and chanted in the synagogue. There are five scrolls which are read on five different feasts: the Song of Songs is read on Passover, the book of Ruth on Shavuot, Lamentations on Tisha B'Av, Ecclesiastes on Sukkot, and Esther on Purim. Though the first four scrolls have a tangential relationship to their feasts, the book of Esther is the very reason for the feast of Purim.

The heroes of the story are Esther, a beautiful young Jewish woman living in Persia, and her cousin Mordecai, who raised her as if she were his daughter. When Esther was taken to the palace of the king of Persia to become part of his harem, the king loved her more than the other women and made Esther queen. The king did not know, however, that Esther was a Jew because Mordecai told her not to reveal her identity.

The villain of the story is Haman, an egotistical advisor to the king. Haman hated Mordecai because Mordecai refused to bow down to Haman, so Haman plotted to kill Mordecai and exterminate all the Jews living in the land. The king handed over the fate of the Jewish people to Haman, to do as he pleased. But Mordecai persuaded Esther to speak to the king on behalf of the Jewish people. Esther prepared herself by fasting for three days, and then went into the king. When she told the king of Haman's plot against her people, the Jewish people were saved and Haman was hanged on the gallows that had been prepared for Mordecai.

During the reading of the scroll in the synagogue on the feast of Purim, it is customary to boo, hiss, stamp feet, and rattle noisemakers whenever the reader mentions the villain's name. So the first two chapter are chanted solemnly enough, but the congregation, especially the children, are poised and waiting. The reader comes to the long-awaited sentence, "After these things King Ahasuerus promoted Haman…" (3:1). The name "Haman" triggers stomping, pounding, and a barrage of whirling rattles. When the ruckus dies down, the reader continues to chant until he comes to another "Haman." The pandemonium breaks loose again. The reading continues, and since Haman soon becomes a chief figure in the story, the explosive racket becomes frequent. The idea is to "blot out the name of Haman," and the youngsters relish the opportunity.

The comic spirit that pervades the reading of the Esther scroll and the upside-down release that characterizes the remainder of the feast are symptoms of Judaism's vitality. Purim is a time for merriment, parties, lampooning skits, and masquerades. Though there is always a serious message behind the happy smile of Purim, the religious obligation to have fun has something very important to teach our modern culture. The topsy-turvy antics of the day express the fact that God is always reversing expectations, lifting up the lowly and crowning his people with unanticipated blessings.

Reflection and discussion

• In what ways is the fate of the Jewish people reversed in the story of Esther?

• What makes Haman such a villian? How might it feel to "blot out the name of Haman"?

• In what ways has God reversed my expectations and offered me unanticipated blessings?

• What is the serious message behind the joyful revelry of Purim?

• What are the main lessons the feast of Purim teaches me?

Prayer

King of all nations, you feed the hungry with banquets, make fertile those who are barren, crown the poor with abundance, and give salvation to those condemned. I praise you as the God who reverses expectations and brings unanticipated surprises to all your people.

They took unhewn stones, as the law directs, and built a new altar like the former one. They also rebuilt the sanctuary and the interior of the temple, and consecrated the courts. 1 Macc 4:47–48

The Maccabees Rebuild the Temple's Altar

1 MACCABEES 4:36–51 *36 Then Judas and his brothers said, "See, our enemies are crushed; let us go up to cleanse the sanctuary and dedicate it." 37 So all the army assembled and went up to Mount Zion. 38 There they saw the sanctuary desolate, the altar profaned, and the gates burned. In the courts they saw bushes sprung up as in a thicket, or as on one of the mountains. They saw also the chambers of the priests in ruins. 39 Then they tore their clothes and mourned with great lamentation; they sprinkled themselves with ashes 40 and fell face down on the ground. And when the signal was given with the trumpets, they cried out to Heaven.*

41 Then Judas detailed men to fight against those in the citadel until he had cleansed the sanctuary. 42 He chose blameless priests devoted to the law, 43 and they cleansed the sanctuary and removed the defiled stones to an unclean place. 44 They deliberated what to do about the altar of burnt-offering, which had been profaned. 45 And they thought it best to tear it down, so that it would not be a lasting shame to them that the Gentiles had defiled it. So they tore down the altar, 46 and stored the stones in a convenient place on the temple hill until a prophet should come to tell what to do with them. ⁴⁷*Then they took unhewn stones, as the law directs, and built a new altar like the former one.* ⁴⁸*They also rebuilt the sanctuary and the interior of the temple, and consecrated the courts.* ⁴⁹*They made new holy vessels, and brought the lampstand, the altar of incense, and the table into the temple.* ⁵⁰*Then they offered incense on the altar and lit the lamps on the lampstand, and these gave light in the temple.* ⁵¹*They placed the bread on the table and hung up the curtains. Thus they finished all the work they had undertaken.*

The feast of Hanukkah, in its origin, is the latest and least of the Jewish holidays: latest in the date of its inauguration, and least in term of the rituals prescribed for its observance. It is celebrated on the twenty-fifth day of the month of Chislev (usually in our December), when the days are short and gloomy, and continues for eight days. This minor feast has become more widely observed in modern times because contemporary Jews identify with its themes of religious liberty and Jewish identity and because it is observed around the time of Christmas, though there is no historical relationship to the Christian feast.

The story of Hanukkah's beginning is told in the first and second books of Maccabees. While the land of Israel was occupied by the Syrian Greeks, Antiochus IV sought to impose the Greek religion and culture on the Jews. In 167 B.C., his armies halted the temple services, installed an altar to Zeus in the temple, and appointed priests to offer swine on the altar of sacrifice. Antiochus made it a capital crime to study the Torah, observe the Sabbath, and circumcise Jewish boys. He sent soldiers throughout every village of Judea to enforce his edicts.

When the soldiers reached the town of Modin, an old priest named Mattathias refused to sacrifice to a Greek idol and slew the man who stepped up to offer the sacrifice in this place along with the king's officer. With the rallying cry, "Let everyone who is zealous for the Torah and the covenant come out with me!" Mattathias and his five sons, Jonathan, Simon, Judah, Eleazar, and Yohanan, fled to the caves of the wilderness to begin a guerilla war against the armies of Antiochus. This ragtag band of Jewish fighters led by the Maccabee brothers, as Mattathias' sons came to be called, eventually liberated the land from its occupiers and reclaimed the temple.

The Maccabees cleansed the temple, dismantled the defiled altar, and constructed a new one in its place. They offered incense within the renewed temple, put out the bread on its table, and lit the lamps of the golden menorah, in preparation for the temple's dedication (*hanukkah*). Soon the Maccabees reestablished Jewish religious autonomy and expelled the supporters of Antiochus. For the first time since the Babylonian conquest, they set up an independent Jewish kingdom in the land. Though it lasted less than a hundred years before the Roman empire swallowed it up, the Maccabean victory developed new strength and possibility for the Jewish people to live as a free and independent people.

In this post-Holocaust world, the Jewish people are acutely aware of the issues raised by the historical events associated with Hanukkah: oppression, religious freedom, identity, and independence. Judaism has always been a stumbling block to those movements that desire all people to dissolve into one, indistinguishable culture. Whether those forces be fascism, Marxism, triumphalist Christianity, or modern secularism, Hanukkah represents resistance to the totalitarian forces that always end up oppressing people in the name of one humanity.

Reflection and discussion

• Why is religious liberty so important for the Jewish people?

• What does the story of the Maccabees teach me about the forces today that threaten religious freedom?

• What are the reasons why the minor feast of Hanukkah has become more important in modern times?

• Why do the Jewish people consider it so essential to maintain their religious identity?

• What is my religious identity? How do I maintain it in the midst of social forces that seek to blot it out?

Prayer

God of freedom and life, you called the people of Israel to the distinctive ways of the covenant and directed them to follow your will faithfully. Give me a spirit of courage and dedication as I strive to be devoted to you in a world that challenges my faith.

Then Judas and his brothers and all the assembly of Israel determined that every year at that season the days of dedication of the altar should be observed with joy and gladness for eight days. 1 Macc 4:59

The Feast of Hanukkah Inaugurated

1 MACCABEES 4:52–61 *⁵²Early in the morning on the twenty-fifth day of the ninth month, which is the month of Chislev, in the one hundred and forty-eighth year, ⁵³they rose and offered sacrifice, as the law directs, on the new altar of burnt-offering that they had built. ⁵⁴At the very season and on the very day that the Gentiles had profaned it, it was dedicated with songs and harps and lutes and cymbals. ⁵⁵All the people fell on their faces and worshipped and blessed Heaven, who had prospered them. ⁵⁶So they celebrated the dedication of the altar for eight days, and joyfully offered burnt-offerings; they offered a sacrifice of well-being and a thanksgiving-offering. ⁵⁷They decorated the front of the temple with golden crowns and small shields; they restored the gates and the chambers for the priests, and fitted them with doors. ⁵⁸There was very great joy among the people, and the disgrace brought by the Gentiles was removed.*

⁵⁹Then Judas and his brothers and all the assembly of Israel determined that every year at that season the days of dedication of the altar should be observed with joy and gladness for eight days, beginning with the twenty-fifth day of the month of Chislev.

[60]*At that time they fortified Mount Zion with high walls and strong towers all round, to keep the Gentiles from coming and trampling them down as they had done before.* [61]*Judas stationed a garrison there to guard it; he also fortified Beth-zur to guard it, so that the people might have a stronghold that faced Idumea.*

On the twenty-fifth day of Chislev, B.C. 164, exactly three years after the temple had been desecrated by order of Antiochus, the Maccabees led the ceremonies of temple renewal and the dedication of the altar. On the new altar of sacrifice which they had constructed, proper offerings were made to God. The new dedication feast was celebrated in many ways like the feast of Booths, which was the occasion on which King Solomon dedicated the first temple (1 Kings 8). For eight days the people offered sacrifices and rejoiced with songs and music.

Though we know the historical circumstances in which Hanukkah was decreed as an annual festival for the Jewish people (verse 59), we are not at all clear about what sort of festival it was or with what ceremonies it was observed in its early period. None of the sources in 1 or 2 Maccabees mention what has become the most characteristic feature of Hanukkah, the lighting of the lamps. Though we know that the menorah, the seven-branched candelabra in the temple, was kindled, this was different from the nine-candled *hanukkiah* that later came to be so characteristic of the feast.

The first mention of a name for the festival comes from Josephus, the first-century Jewish historian. He writes that the festival was called "Lights," because, as he said, "freedom glowed and lighted up Jewish life unexpectedly." The rabbis of the time discussed the kindling of the lights for each day of the feast. Followers of Rabbi Shammai stated that the festival must begin with the kindling of eight lights, steadily diminishing the number until there is only one light on the last day. Rabbi Hillel's followers held that the feast should begin with one light and end with eight.

By the second century, the holiday had become known as Hanukkah, or the Feast of Dedication. But it is only in the Talmud, a few centuries later, that we find the famous story of the miraculous flask of oil that lasted for eight days. As the story is told, when the Maccabees entered the temple after its desecration, they could find only one small container of oil bearing the seal of the high priest, enough to light the menorah for only one day. But the oil miraculously lasted for eight days, throughout the festival of Hanukkah.

The only religious ritual belonging to Hanukkah is the lighting of candles. The candles are arranged in a candelabrum called a Hanukkah menorah (or hanukkiah) that holds nine candles: one for each of the eight nights of the feast, plus a shammus (servant) candle at a different height. On the first night, one candle is placed at the far right. The shammus candle is lit and three blessings are recited. The first candle is then lit using the shammus candle, and the shammus candle is placed in its holder. Each night, another candle is added from right to left. But the new candles are lit first, so candles are lit from left to right. Most Hanukkah candles are slender, so they are allowed to burn out on their own and are then replaced the next night. On the eighth night, all nine candles (the eight Hanukkah candles and the shammus) glow.

Hanukkah is primarily a family festival celebrated in the home. Jewish law prohibits work for one hour after candlelighting. This time period is traditionally used for family learning, specifically to teach children about Hanukkah through study and discussion. Families also use this time for games, singing, and gift-giving. The most traditional of the games is called *dreidel*, a gambling game played with a spinning top. Most people play for pennies or M&Ms. The legend says that during the time of persecution under Antiochus, those who wanted to study the Torah had to conceal their illegal activity by playing the spinning game whenever an official was within sight. Another reminder of the miracle of the oil comes through the smells and tastes of oil that permeate special Hanukkah foods, especially the potato latkes (pancakes).

The candles that burn in the windows of Jewish homes are a tribute to religious freedom and the blessings of God. From one century to another, the Jews have been told that there is no more oil left to burn. But Hanukkah proclaims that God's people do not surrender to the night or curse the darkness. They always light another candle.

Reflection and discussion

• What is the meaning of the candles lit for the days of Hanukkah?

• What was the purpose in dedicating the new altar of the temple? Why are religious objects often blessed or devoted to God with religious ritual?

• Why is dreidel a traditional game associated with the days of Hanukkah?

• Why does the family-centered teaching and leisure of Hanukkah contrast so sharply with our consumer-driven culture in December? What can the spirit of Hanukkah teach me?

Prayer

Lord of Light, you brighten the darkness of gloomy seasons and enlighten the world with hope. Illuminate the shadows of my life so that I may live in genuine freedom and witness your covenant to all the nations.

It happened that on the same day on which the sanctuary had been profaned by the foreigners, the purification of the sanctuary took place, that is,
on the twenty-fifth day of the same month, which was Chislev. 2 Macc 10:5

Eight Days of Rejoicing

2 MACCABEES 10:1–8 ¹*Now Maccabeus and his followers, the Lord leading them on, recovered the temple and the city; ²they tore down the altars that had
been built in the public square by the foreigners, and also destroyed the sacred
precincts. ³They purified the sanctuary, and made another altar of sacrifice; then,
striking fire out of flint, they offered sacrifices, after a lapse of two years, and they
offered incense and lighted lamps and set out the bread of the Presence. ⁴When
they had done this, they fell prostrate and implored the Lord that they might
never again fall into such misfortunes, but that, if they should ever sin, they might
be disciplined by him with forbearance and not be handed over to blasphemous
and barbarous nations. ⁵It happened that on the same day on which the sanctuary had been profaned by the foreigners, the purification of the sanctuary took
place, that is, on the twenty-fifth day of the same month, which was Chislev.
⁶They celebrated it for eight days with rejoicing, in the manner of the festival of
booths, remembering how not long before, during the festival of booths, they had
been wandering in the mountains and caves like wild animals. ⁷Therefore, carrying ivy-wreathed wands and beautiful branches and also fronds of palm, they
offered hymns of thanksgiving to him who had given success to the purifying of*

*his own holy place. *[8]*They decreed by public edict, ratified by vote, that the whole nation of the Jews should observe these days every year.*

The winter month of December, when the days are shortest, is the season of light in many ancient cultures. The ancient Yule celebrations lit oil lamps around the time of the winter solstice. The candles and lights of Advent and Christmas continue this practice of expressing the growing light that emerges from the darkness. Likewise, Hanukkah celebrates the light of hope born from the darkness of despair. At the gloomiest time of Jewish history, the spark of the Maccabean rebellion fanned into flame. In a darkened temple, the Jews lit the lamps that wondrously burned for eight days. Hanukkah is about transcending the darkness with courage, fidelity, and hope.

It is ironic that the feast that celebrates Judaism's religious freedom and unique identity is the one that has been most absorbed into the dominant culture of the majority. As a minor feast in Judaism's annual cycle of holidays, Hanukkah can't hold a candle to Christmas. So as not to let their children feel deprived, many Jews have introduced gift-giving and other Christmas customs into their celebration of Hanukkah. But those Jewish parents who are most perceptive gather their children around the radiant hanukkiah and tell them their courageous history, about a rich tradition that could have flickered and gone out centuries ago but still continues to burn. While the mass marketers expand the purchasing month of December and try to inflate Hanukkah as the Jewish alternative to Christmas, the wise parents tell their children, "We're Jewish—we have Hanukkah, Passover, Shavuot, Sukkot, Simchat Torah, Purim, and most importantly, Shabbat every week." Children who have experienced the building of a sukkah will not feel disadvantaged when they don't decorate a Christmas tree. Those who have shared a Passover Seder will not feel deprived of a Christmas dinner. When children have given and received gifts on Purim, paraded with the holy scrolls on Simchat Torah, brought first fruits at Shavuot, and welcomed the Sabbath each week with candles and good food, they will know that to be Jewish means having a calendar full of joyful celebrations. Those same children will soon understand that if their ancestors had not stood firm and Antiochus IV had succeeded in obliterating Judaism, there would be no Christmas at all. Without the victory of Hanukkah, Christians would not be able to sing, "born is the king of Israel."

After narrating the deeds of Jesus on the feasts of Passover and Booths, John's gospel tells us that Jesus was walking in the temple on the occasion of the mid-winter festival of Dedication (Hanukkah; John 10:22). The feast summoned the Jewish people to look to the temple as the visible manifestation of God's presence and to remain faithful to their identity as people of the covenant. But a generation after Jesus, as the temple lay in ruin, Jewish Christianity and rabbinical Judaism struggled with how to maintain the tradition of Israel without the temple. John's gospel identified Jesus as the new temple, the completion of God's presence among his people because of the oneness between Jesus and the Father. It is no longer necessary to seek God in the holy temple and the consecrated altar; God is made known in "the one whom the Father has sanctified" (John 10:36). Proud of their heritage in ancient Israel, the early Christians realized that the festive celebrations of Judaism express the longings that are fulfilled in Jesus, the Jewish Messiah.

Reflection and discussion

• Why are winter festivals so often identified with lights and candles? What are some examples?

• In what ways do Jews maintain the distinctiveness of Hanukkah in the midst of the holiday culture of December?

• What is the difference between the traditional seven-branched menorah and the hanukkiah?

• What do I think Rabbi Heschel mean when he described the Jewish feasts as "sanctuaries in time"?

• In what sense can I say that the Jewish people are my elder brothers and sisters?

Prayer

Lord God, teach me to long for your presence and keep me faithful to your covenant. Give me a deep love for the traditions of ancient Israel and a true gratitude for the faith of my spiritual ancestors. Help me to keep the flame of faith alive in my heart.

SUGGESTIONS FOR FACILITATORS, GROUP SESSION 5

1. Welcome group members and ask if anyone has any questions, announcements, or requests.

2. You may want to pray this prayer as a group:

Lord God, you lift your people from certain death and sustain them when all seems lost. As we study the feasts of the Ninth of Av, Purim, and Hanukkah, help us to believe in your promises and trust in your faithfulness. Help us to hear the cries of your suffering people and to be instruments of your mercy to those in need. Through our study of these feasts, shake up our routine expectations and bring us surprising graces. Give us commitment and courage as we strive to manifest your presence in a darkened world.

3. Ask one or more of the following questions:

   • What most intrigued you from this week's study?
   • What makes you want to know and understand more of God's word?

4. Discuss lessons 19 through 24. Choose one or more of the questions for reflection and discussion from each lesson to talk over as a group.

5. Ask the group members to name one thing they have most appreciated about the way the group has worked during this Bible study. Ask group members to discuss any changes they might suggest in the way the group works in future studies.

6. Invite group members to complete lessons 25 through 30 on their own during the six days before the next meeting. They should write out their own answers to the questions as preparation for next week's session.

7. Discuss examples of how the words and images of Judaism's feasts have influenced your understanding of religious practice and ritual.

8. Conclude by praying aloud together the prayer at the end of one of the lessons discussed. You may want to conclude the prayer by asking members to voice prayers of thanksgiving.

Six days you shall labor and do all your work. But the seventh day is a sabbath to the Lord your God; you shall not do any work. Deut 5:13–14

Honor the Sabbath Day

EXODUS 20:8–11 *⁸Remember the sabbath day, and keep it holy. ⁹Six days you shall labor and do all your work. ¹⁰But the seventh day is a sabbath to the Lord your God; you shall not do any work—you, your son or your daughter, your male or female slave, your livestock, or the alien resident in your towns. ¹¹For in six days the Lord made heaven and earth, the sea, and all that is in them, but rested the seventh day; therefore the Lord blessed the sabbath day and consecrated it.*

DEUTERONOMY 5:12–15 *¹²Observe the sabbath day and keep it holy, as the Lord your God commanded you. ¹³Six days you shall labor and do all your work. ¹⁴But the seventh day is a sabbath to the Lord your God; you shall not do any work—you, or your son or your daughter, or your male or female slave, or your ox or your donkey, or any of your livestock, or the resident alien in your towns, so that your male and female slave may rest as well as you. ¹⁵Remember that you were a slave in the land of Egypt, and the Lord your God brought you out from there with a mighty hand and an outstretched arm; therefore the Lord your God commanded you to keep the sabbath day.*

The Sabbath is the most important observance in Judaism, the only ritual feast instituted in the Ten Commandments. Observant Jews look upon the Sabbath as a gift from God, a day that they joyfully await throughout the week. It is a time for setting aside weekday concerns and devoting oneself to higher pursuits.

Western society has become so accustomed to a weekend break that we don't realize what a radical concept a day of rest was in ancient times. A weekly day of rest has no parallel in any other ancient culture, and can rightly be called one of the great gifts of Israelite culture to human civilization. While other societies divided work and leisure along class lines, leisure being reserved for the ruling classes and never for the laboring classes, the Jewish Sabbath divides work and leisure in time: "Six days you shall labor and do all your work. But the seventh day is a sabbath to the Lord your God" (Exod 20:9–10; Deut 5:13–14).

The primary character of the Sabbath is rest. It provides for a cyclical release from the tyranny of unrelenting, ceaseless labor. Yet, the Sabbath is not just a holiday to rest up for another week of work. The Israelites are commanded to keep the Sabbath holy. In biblical Hebrew, "holy" means withdrawn from common use and reserved for a special purpose associated with God. The Sabbath is a day consecrated to God in a special way.

The two versions of the Ten Commandments give us two different motivations for obeying the Sabbath law. The Exodus account places the Sabbath in the context of God's creation: "For in six days the Lord made heaven and earth, the sea, and all that is in them, but rested the seventh day" (Exod 20:11). By resting on the seventh day and sanctifying it, we acknowledge that God is the creator of all things and that all of our labor must fit into God's purposes for the world. In the account of Deuteronomy, the Sabbath is placed in the context of God's liberation of the Israelites from slavery: "Remember that you were a slave in the land of Egypt, and the Lord your God brought you out from there with a mighty hand and an outstretched arm; therefore the Lord your God commanded you to keep the sabbath day" (Deut 5:15). Resting on the Sabbath is a reminder that God's people are no longer slaves, but are truly free. Breaking free from labor reminds them that God broke them free from endless toil and bondage. Thus, according to the texts of the Ten Commandments, Sabbath is a weekly reminder that God is both creator and liberator, and it is an opportunity to honor the God of life and freedom.

The two versions of the command insist that the gift of the Sabbath is for all, especially for those who might not easily find rest. It has been called history's first and greatest worker protection act. The texts maintain that the Sabbath is for both men and women, for landowners and slaves, for Israelites and foreigners, for humans and even the animals. The divisions and distinctions that human striving has erected are broken down on the Sabbath. The seventh day anticipates a new creation when the world's creatures will again be at peace with one another and God will be able to look again upon his creation and pronounce it "very good" (Gen 1:31).

Reflection and discussion

• The Torah identifies holy people, holy places, and holy time. What does it mean to keep the Sabbath holy?

• In what way is the motivation for keeping the Sabbath different in Exodus and Deuteronomy?

• How does the Sabbath promote justice and protection for all God's creatures?

• What do I appreciate most about the weekend? Why is leisure so essential in every human life?

• What can I do to sanctify a day of leisure, worship, and spiritual study in my life?

Prayer

Creator and Redeemer, you call your people to respect the created rhythm of work and leisure. Teach me to how to work well and to rest well, always grateful for your blessings. Make me an instrument of your justice in the world.

The Israelites shall keep the sabbath, observing the sabbath throughout their generations, as a perpetual covenant. It is a sign forever between me and the people of Israel. Exod 31:16–17

The Sabbath of Solemn Rest

EXODUS 31:12–17 *¹²The Lord said to Moses: ¹³You yourself are to speak to the Israelites: "You shall keep my sabbaths, for this is a sign between me and you throughout your generations, given in order that you may know that I, the Lord, sanctify you. ¹⁴You shall keep the sabbath, because it is holy for you; everyone who profanes it shall be put to death; whoever does any work on it shall be cut off from among the people. ¹⁵Six days shall work be done, but the seventh day is a sabbath of solemn rest, holy to the Lord; whoever does any work on the sabbath day shall be put to death. ¹⁶Therefore the Israelites shall keep the sabbath, observing the sabbath throughout their generations, as a perpetual covenant. ¹⁷It is a sign forever between me and the people of Israel that in six days the Lord made heaven and earth, and on the seventh day he rested, and was refreshed."*

These instructions to observe the Sabbath come at the end of God's establishment of his covenant with Israel on Mount Sinai (Exod 19–31). The Sabbath is to be a special "sign" between God and his people (verses 13, 17), a weekly reminder and expression of the covenant. By keeping the Sabbath, the Israelites would perpetually demonstrate that they were sanctified by God to be his "treasured possession…a priestly kingdom and a holy nation" (19:5–6).

God built a rhythm of working and resting into the created order (verse 17). So, honoring the Sabbath is a participation in God's intention for creation. Not keeping the Sabbath is a violation of God's created order and contributes to the regression of creation and its return to chaos. The harsh penalties associated with violations of the Sabbath indicate the seriousness of the covenant and the Sabbath's place at the heart of God's design.

When we fail to see our work within the context of its God-given role, we alienate ourselves from God as the source of our fulfillment. Our work and the material benefits it generates can dominate the whole of life and define our very being. We begin to believe that what we do defines who we are. Work becomes an idol to be served without regard for God's claim on our lives.

Sabbath-keeping provides for a weekly oasis, reminding us that God is in charge of creation, not us. It released us from our schedules and deadlines and relentless pursuits. We are forced to pause and remind ourselves that time, too, belongs to God. On the Sabbath, we are freed from our jobs, our creditors, and our need to provide for ourselves. All human striving is put aside in order to honor God as the source of our lives and to recognize his purposes as our fulfillment.

Jewish tradition developed the custom of welcoming the Sabbath as a weekly home ritual on Friday evenings. The Jewish home is as important as the synagogue; it is the place where spirituality is lived and passed onto the next generation. The house is cleaned and the Sabbath meals prepared in advance, in order to enjoy a Sabbath free of chores. Just before sundown, the Sabbath candles are lit and a blessing recited, usually by the woman of the house. Before the family meal, parents bless their children one-by-one by laying their hands upon their children's heads, offering a prayer, and kissing them on their forehead.

As families sit down for the Sabbath meal, the man of the house recites Kiddush, a prayer sanctifying the Sabbath, over a cup of wine. After the ritual hand-washing, the meal is shared in a spirit of joy and festivity. Two twisted loaves of freshly-baked bread remind the family of the double portion of manna given by God in the wilderness on the Sabbath. Even the poorest try to serve special food and invite a guest to the Sabbath table. Special hymns are sung and the entire evening should be one of pleasure, relaxation, and ease.

The Sabbath is devoted to holy activities, which often people have no time for during the week, especially study and prayer. The study of Scripture is most important for the Sabbath, and often Jews will go to the synagogue. The traditional Sabbath greeting is "Shabbat shalom," a wish for a good and peaceful Sabbath. Two more meals are eaten on the day of Sabbath, with the third Sabbath meal closing the day of rest.

The departure of the Sabbath is marked by a brief ritual called Havdalah. The word literally means "distinction" or "separation," which is exactly what it accomplishes. It marks the transition from the holiness of the Sabbath to the ordinariness of weekdays. Traditionally, the Sabbath ends when three stars appear in the sky on Saturday night. At Havdalah, the family says farewell to the Sabbath with the hope that the peace of the day will remain during the week. The ritual is recited with a cup of wine, a container of spices, and a braided Havdalah candle. The blessing over the wine sanctifies the moment and sniffing the spices is a gentle awakening to earthly responsibilities and a reminder to carry the sweet spice of Sabbath into the week. The lighting of the candle is a reminder of God's separation of the light and darkness on the first day of the week and an encouragement to begin again to share in God's work of creation. The candle is then doused and everyone wishes each other a good week. Havdalah demonstrates that while Shabbat is a taste of the perfection to come, our weekday work in the world is necessary to bring it about.

Reflection and discussion

• In what way is the Sabbath a "sign" of the covenant between God and his people?

• How is the Sabbath an expression of God's concern for our mental health and personal satisfaction?

• Do I create a healthy rhythm of work and leisure? What can I do to create a regular oasis of rest in my life?

• Why is the home as important as the synagogue for Jewish faith formation? How can I create a household of faith?

Prayer

Blessed are you, Lord God of all creation, through your goodness you have given the Sabbath as a refuge of rest and joy in our anxious world. Teach me to observe the rhythm of work and leisure so that my life will always reflect your gift of freedom.

For the sake of your lives, take care that you do not bear a burden on the sabbath day or bring it in by the gates of Jerusalem. And do not carry a burden out of your houses on the sabbath or do any work, but keep the sabbath day holy, as I commanded your ancestors. Jer 17:21–22

Call the Sabbath a Delight

ISAIAH 58:13–14

¹³*If you refrain from trampling the sabbath,*
from pursuing your own interests on my holy day;
if you call the sabbath a delight
and the holy day of the Lord honorable;
if you honor it, not going your own ways,
serving your own interests, or pursuing your own affairs;
¹⁴*then you shall take delight in the Lord,*
and I will make you ride upon the heights of the earth;
I will feed you with the heritage of your ancestor Jacob,
for the mouth of the Lord has spoken.

JEREMIAH 17:19–27   ¹⁹*Thus said the Lord to me: Go and stand in the People's Gate, by which the kings of Judah enter and by which they go out, and in all the gates of Jerusalem,* ²⁰*and say to them: Hear the word of the Lord, you kings*

of Judah, and all Judah, and all the inhabitants of Jerusalem, who enter by these gates. ²¹Thus says the Lord: For the sake of your lives, take care that you do not bear a burden on the sabbath day or bring it in by the gates of Jerusalem. ²²And do not carry a burden out of your houses on the sabbath or do any work, but keep the sabbath day holy, as I commanded your ancestors. ²³Yet they did not listen or incline their ear; they stiffened their necks and would not hear or receive instruction.

²⁴But if you listen to me, says the Lord, and bring in no burden by the gates of this city on the sabbath day, but keep the sabbath day holy and do no work on it, ²⁵then there shall enter by the gates of this city kings who sit on the throne of David, riding in chariots and on horses, they and their officials, the people of Judah and the inhabitants of Jerusalem; and this city shall be inhabited forever. ²⁶And people shall come from the towns of Judah and the places around Jerusalem, from the land of Benjamin, from the Shephelah, from the hill country, and from the Negeb, bringing burnt offerings and sacrifices, grain offerings and frankincense, and bringing thank offerings to the house of the Lord. ²⁷But if you do not listen to me, to keep the sabbath day holy, and to carry in no burden through the gates of Jerusalem on the sabbath day, then I will kindle a fire in its gates; it shall devour the palaces of Jerusalem and shall not be quenched.

Sabbath observance united the Israelites as a people, celebrated their identity, and expressed their relationship with God. As the regulations for the Sabbath developed through the centuries, they expanded along two lines: the restrictive and the affirmative. On the one hand, the Sabbath laws grew in number in order to eliminate all forms of work and insure external rest. On the other hand, the teachings on the Sabbath emphasized internal rest, spiritual renewal, and joyful leisure. As these two dimensions of the Sabbath grew simultaneously, the Scriptures speak of honoring the Sabbath as a joy and "delight" (Isa 58:13), not as a restrictive burden.

In order to insure rest, specific types of work were prohibited. It was forbidden to gather wood (Num 15:32), to light fires (Exod 35:3), to prepare food (Exod 16:23), or to move unnecessarily from place to place (Exod 16:29). Isaiah warned the people against doing business on the Sabbath (Isa 58:13), and Jeremiah cautioned them not to carry anything to and from their homes and not to do any work (Jer 17:21–22). Yet, these restrictions were not designed to simply create a day off. Rather, they set off an entire day, from sundown on Friday to twilight on Saturday evening, as time apart from daily existence, dedicated to ennobled pleasure.

The Jewish tradition continued to expand the theological themes of Sabbath through the centuries. According to the Talmud, the rabbis used to dress in the white garments of a bridegroom in order to greet the Sabbath bride. The liturgical poem "Lecha Dodi" ("come my beloved") is still sung on Friday evenings in the synagogue. Jewish mysticism associated Sabbath with the feminine presence of God, called the Shechinah, or "in-dwelling" of God. The Sabbath was thought of as a day of mystical union between the Jewish people and God. Reflecting the intimacy of this spiritual union, some texts speak of the Sabbath as an especially promising day for a husband and wife to be intimate with one another, as a symbolic union of God and God's beloved people.

The Talmud says that two angels accompany all Jews to their homes on Friday evenings. So the Sabbath observance begins with the song "Shalom Aleichem," a hymn welcoming the angels as guests and announcing the arrival of the Sabbath bride. Through these and many other traditions and rituals, the Jewish people have transformed what might otherwise be a day of mere inactivity into one of joy, holiness, and peace. Truly the Sabbath is the hallmark and crowning glory of Jewish culture.

Reflection and discussion

• How do the Jewish people transform the multiple prohibitions of the Sabbath into an experience of joyful delight?

• What can the Jewish tradition teach me about the purpose of laws and regulations in safeguarding religious tradition?

• Why do the Jewish people often read the love poetry of the Song of Songs on Friday evening? What can I learn from the Jewish tradition about the unity of sexual intimacy and one's relationship with God?

• Do I consider my religious life a pleasure and a delight? How does God want me to experience my relationship with him?

Prayer

Lord of the universe, you created the world and gave your people the holy rest of the Sabbath. Teach me to honor your gift of leisure and free me from the compulsion of restless activity. Show me how to delight in the rest of Sabbath peace.

Six years you shall sow your field, and six years you shall prune your vineyard, and gather in their yield; but in the seventh year there shall be a sabbath of complete rest for the land, a sabbath for the Lord: you shall not sow your field or prune your vineyard. Lev 25:3-4

The Sabbatical Year

LEVITICUS 25:1–7 *¹The Lord spoke to Moses on Mount Sinai, saying: ²Speak to the people of Israel and say to them: When you enter the land that I am giving you, the land shall observe a sabbath for the Lord. ³Six years you shall sow your field, and six years you shall prune your vineyard, and gather in their yield; ⁴but in the seventh year there shall be a sabbath of complete rest for the land, a sabbath for the Lord: you shall not sow your field or prune your vineyard. ⁵You shall not reap the aftergrowth of your harvest or gather the grapes of your unpruned vine: it shall be a year of complete rest for the land. ⁶You may eat what the land yields during its sabbath—you, your male and female slaves, your hired and your bound laborers who live with you; ⁷for your livestock also, and for the wild animals in your land all its yield shall be for food.*

DEUTERONOMY 15:1–11 *¹Every seventh year you shall grant a remission of debts. ²And this is the manner of the remission: every creditor shall remit the claim that is held against a neighbor, not exacting it of a neighbor who is a member of the* *community, because the Lord's remission has been proclaimed. ³Of a foreigner you may exact it, but you must remit your claim on whatever any member of your community owes you. ⁴There will, however, be no one in need among you, because the Lord is sure to bless you in the land that the Lord your God is giving you as a possession to occupy, ⁵if only you will obey the Lord your God by diligently observing this entire commandment that I command you today. ⁶When the Lord your God has blessed you, as he promised you, you will lend to many nations, but you will not borrow; you will rule over many nations, but they will not rule over you.*

⁷If there is among you anyone in need, a member of your community in any of your towns within the land that the Lord your God is giving you, do not be hardhearted or tight-fisted toward your needy neighbor. ⁸You should rather open your hand, willingly lending enough to meet the need, whatever it may be. ⁹Be careful that you do not entertain a mean thought, thinking, "The seventh year, the year of remission, is near," and therefore view your needy neighbor with hostility and give nothing; your neighbor might cry to the Lord against you, and you would incur guilt. ¹⁰Give liberally and be ungrudging when you do so, for on this account the Lord your God will bless you in all your work and in all that you undertake. ¹¹Since there will never cease to be some in need on the earth, I therefore command you, "Open your hand to the poor and needy neighbor in your land."

Just as the seventh day of the week is the Sabbath, the seventh year in a continuous cycle of years is called the sabbatical year. The Sabbath principle of honoring God's creation and God's gift of freedom is extended into the whole seventh year, "a sabbath of complete rest for the land" (Lev 25:4-5). In this seventh year, the sowing and reaping of the fields, as well as the pruning and picking of vines, are prohibited. After six years of being worked, the land is to enjoy rest.

For an agricultural society, the Sabbath of the land was also a year-long sabbatical for the populace. In the sabbatical year, the whole society lived at a significantly lower standard of living in order to release itself from the daily grind and devote itself to higher pursuits. Though this ancient institution seems incredible in today's hurried society, equally amazing is the humanitarian and egalitarian nature of the sabbatical year. All the produce of the land that grew naturally during the fallow year was free to all, including hired workers, aliens, slaves, and even animals.

The book of Deuteronomy expands the sabbatical year from the agricultural sphere into the economic sphere. Not only does the legislation include a year of release for the land, but also a release from the burden of debt. In the seventh year, all loans are to be forgiven, allowing people sunk in debt an opportunity to start over. This year of liberation for the land and for debtors is rooted in Israel's understanding that God is the true owner of the land. God said, "The land is mine, with me you are but aliens and tenants" (Lev 25:23). Therefore, everything that pertains to the use and ownership of the land has ethical implications and falls within the concerns of Israel's covenant with God.

The biblical pattern encourages hard work, getting ahead, ownership, and expansion. But it insists on pauses for rest. Every seventh day, all the work must stop; every seventh year, people are forbidden to get ahead by working the land and those who have become enslaved by debt must be set free. For people and for the land, overwork leads to exhaustion. Periodic times of fallowness are vital for continued fertility and productivity. We need periods of rest and renewal, and when we pause to revitalize, everyone benefits. The biblical Sabbath teaches us that our wealth, land, and possessions are not private property to be accumulated, but divine gifts channeled through us to be shared for the benefit of all.

The ancient sabbatical year is continued today in the practice of allowing academics and other professionals a time for leisure and learning every seven years. Yet, the original sabbatical was not for elite specialists, but for farmers. The sabbatical principle urges us to demand alternatives to society's unfettered production and consumption. By dictating periods of enforced regeneration, rededication and redistribution, the sabbatical year presents a compelling alternative to life's relentless pace and continuous toil. By breaking with life's ordinary routine, it creates spaces in life for higher pursuits.

Today, as ecologists and economists try to figure out how to create a just society and a sustainable economy, the Sabbath offers a reasonable direction. It encourages us to gain control over the frenetic pace of economic expansion and technological development. It urges us to pause and reflect on spiritual and moral values, to refuse to allow expansion to outstrip ethical deliberation. It shows us that an economy disengaged from social and environmental concerns will deplete the earth and drain human energies. It encourages rich societies to remit the enslaving debts of poor nations, because a just world is one in which all people participate.

The Sabbath principle is an urgent message from an ancient time that can provide a much-needed challenge and hope for our culture. While the specific solutions of ancient Israel may be deemed impractical for our society and our lifestyles, the principles of the seventh day and the seventh year—resting, reflecting, releasing—can point our way to a more hopeful future.

Reflection and discussion

• The sabbatical year is called the year of "release" in the Jewish tradition. What are the benefits of a year of release?

• If God is the true owner of the earth and we are God's tenants, what does this imply about our concerns and responsibilities in the world?

• How can the Jewish tradition of the Sabbath year lead to new ways of thinking about social and environmental problems today?

Prayer

Lord of all the earth, you are the creator and owner of the whole world. As a tenant on your land, I am a steward of the good things you have given me. Give me a deep respect and concern for the earth and all its creatures

That fiftieth year shall be a jubilee for you: you shall not sow, or reap the aftergrowth, or harvest the unpruned vines. For it is a jubilee; it shall be holy to you: you shall eat only what the field itself produces. Lev 25:11–12

The Year of Jubilee

LEVITICUS 25:8–17 ⁸ *You shall count off seven weeks of years, seven times seven years, so that the period of seven weeks of years gives forty-nine years.* ⁹ *Then you shall have the trumpet sounded loud; on the tenth day of the seventh month—on the day of atonement—you shall have the trumpet sounded throughout all your land.* ¹⁰ *And you shall hallow the fiftieth year and you shall proclaim liberty throughout the land to all its inhabitants. It shall be a jubilee for you: you shall return, every one of you, to your property and every one of you to your family.* ¹¹ *That fiftieth year shall be a jubilee for you: you shall not sow, or reap the aftergrowth, or harvest the unpruned vines.* ¹² *For it is a jubilee; it shall be holy to you: you shall eat only what the field itself produces.*

¹³ *In this year of jubilee you shall return, every one of you, to your property.* ¹⁴ *When you make a sale to your neighbor or buy from your neighbor, you shall not cheat one another.* ¹⁵ *When you buy from your neighbor, you shall pay only for the number of years since the jubilee; the seller shall charge you only for the remaining crop years.* ¹⁶ *If the years are more, you shall increase the price, and if the years are fewer, you shall diminish the price; for it is a certain number of harvests that are being sold to you.* ¹⁷ *You shall not cheat one another, but you shall fear your God; for I am the Lord your God.*

The Torah states that the year of Jubilee was to occur every fifty years. It is the final extension of the Sabbath principle, which began with the day of rest every seventh day, extended to the Sabbath of the land every seventh year, and then lastly to the Jubilee, which followed seven cycles of seven years (forty-nine years). The fiftieth year, or Jubilee, began on the Day of Atonement, and was proclaimed by the blowing of the ram's horn (verse 9). The Jubilee was a holy year, a year characterized by freedom for all: "You shall hallow the fiftieth year and you shall proclaim liberty throughout the land to all its inhabitants" (verse 10). During the Jubilee all Israelites slaves were to be freed, the land was to lie fallow, and ancestral lands that had been sold during the preceding fifty years were to be redeemed by the family of their original owners.

The purpose of the Jubilee laws was to promote justice within society. Compliance would prevent the development of a permanent landless class or a permanent class of slaves. In a society without economic controls, the tendency is for the rich to get richer, because they have the means to produce wealth, and for the poor to get poorer, because they are deprived of such means and are perpetually dependent. By redistributing the land and freeing slaves once every generation, the community would share land more equitably and prevent the accumulation of ownership in the hands of a wealthy few. Israel's ideal was to have neither extremely wealthy land owners nor extremely poor landless people, but for every family to have land sufficient to meet its basic needs. The economic collapse of a family in one generation should not condemn all future generations to the bondage of perpetual indebtedness.

There is no evidence that the year of Jubilee was ever actually put into practice in ancient Israel. However, the Jubilee ideal continued in Israel's imagination and entered the prophetic writings as a vision for the future. Most clearly, Isaiah 61 used images of the Jubilee to express Israel's hopes for the days to come. The one whom God would anoint with his own Spirit would proclaim "liberty to the captives and release to the prisoners" (Isa 61:1). The language of the Jubilee portrayed God's future messianic redemption, "the year of the Lord's favor" (Isa 61:2).

In the synagogue of Nazareth, Jesus announced that Israel's hopes for its final restoration were being fulfilled in his own ministry (Luke 4:16–21). Reading from the scroll of Isaiah 61, he proclaimed the coming of God's kingdom, using the Jubilee as the model. The time for repentance had come, and the release assured in the Jubilee would unfold throughout his ministry.

Release from bondage, freedom from oppression, the opportunity to begin again—these are the deep hopes of the Jubilee manifested through the coming of the Messiah.

Reflection and discussion

• Why did the year of Jubilee begin on the Day of Atonement? How can a conversion of people's hearts lead to social change?

• If the Jubilee year was implemented in our society today, what would be the results of such radical changes?

• Why did Jesus proclaim the inauguration of his ministry with the words of Isaiah 61? In what way is the kingdom of God the fullness of the Jubilee?

Prayer

Merciful God, you bring liberty to captives and release to prisoners. You forgive the debts and sins of your people, and you give us the opportunity to begin again. Free me from bondage and make me an instrument of your justice in the world.

Then he said to them, "The sabbath was made for humankind, and not humankind for the sabbath; so the Son of Man is lord even of the sabbath."

Mark 2:27–28

Lord Even of the Sabbath

MARK 2:23—3:6 ²³*One sabbath he was going through the grainfields; and as they made their way his disciples began to pluck heads of grain.* ²⁴*The Pharisees said to him, "Look, why are they doing what is not lawful on the sabbath?"* ²⁵*And he said to them, "Have you never read what David did when he and his companions were hungry and in need of food?* ²⁶*He entered the house of God, when Abiathar was high priest, and ate the bread of the Presence, which it is not lawful for any but the priests to eat, and he gave some to his companions."* ²⁷*Then he said to them, "The sabbath was made for humankind, and not humankind for the sabbath;* ²⁸*so the Son of Man is lord even of the sabbath."*

3 ¹*Again he entered the synagogue, and a man was there who had a withered hand.* ²*They watched him to see whether he would cure him on the sabbath, so that they might accuse him.* ³*And he said to the man who had the withered hand, "Come forward."* ⁴*Then he said to them, "Is it lawful to do good or to do harm on the sabbath, to save life or to kill?" But they were silent.* ⁵*He looked around at them with anger; he was grieved at their hardness of heart and said to the man, "Stretch out your hand." He stretched it out, and his hand was restored.* ⁶*The Pharisees went out and immediately conspired with the Herodians against him, how to destroy him.*

In the days of Jesus, observance of the Sabbath was a supremely important demonstration of loyalty to Judaism and its covenant with God. The gospels clearly demonstrate that Jesus and his followers, as faithful Jews, honored the Sabbath, and the early Christians also continued to keep the Sabbath and attend synagogue services on the Sabbath. For this reason, the gospel accounts in which Jesus and his disciples are accused of dishonoring the Sabbath by traveling, gathering food, and healing are not just controversies about scrupulous observance. Rather, they indicate that the final purpose of the Sabbath, the coming of God's kingdom, has arrived.

Certainly opinions varied during the time of the Second Temple about what was allowable on the Sabbath. The rabbis would later codify in the Talmud thirty-nine different prohibitions in order to safeguard the sanctity of the Sabbath as a day of complete rest. However, all the restrictive laws of the Sabbath vanished in the presence of human emergency: disaster, self-defense, peril to life and limb, and the like. There were lots of moderations in the rigorous Sabbath rest, and Jesus affirmed a principle that most Jews already understood when he stated that the Sabbath was made for humankind, or as a later rabbi of the second century wrote, "The Sabbath was delivered to you, and not you to the Sabbath."

Jesus' teaching about the Sabbath related to the Jewish belief that the Sabbath anticipated the messianic age. Jewish teaching emphasized that the Sabbath was a foretaste of God's kingdom, an anticipation in the present world of the world to come. The coming day of perfect peace, healing, wholeness, and joy was foreshadowed in God's gift of the Sabbath. Therefore, the rabbis taught that people should conduct themselves on the Sabbath as if the future time were already at hand.

The defense Jesus offered when his followers were accused of traveling and picking grain on the Sabbath is related to the urgency of their ministry in proclaiming the kingdom of God. Jesus showed that David's breach of religious rules was necessitated by the divine mission David had received. David was the great king of ancient Israel, the one from whom the Messiah would descend. The text presents the calling and mission of Jesus as the long-expected king, the Messiah who would fulfill the deepest hopes of Israel.

Jesus' Sabbath healing was likewise a sign and foretaste of the kingdom he confidently announced. Jesus healed on the Sabbath, not to violate the law or to show he was above the law, but to link his healing with that day which symbolized the future kingdom he had come to bring. With Jesus, the kingdom was at hand, and he came to bring the renewal, wholeness, and blessedness that had long been associated with the Sabbath.

Jesus is "lord even of the Sabbath" (verse 28) because he came to bring the divine gifts that were foreshadowed in the Sabbath. That day—when all human infirmities will be healed, all oppression lifted, and all in bondage released—was coming into the world in him. His urgent work on the Sabbath forced his audience to make a decision: either he was the one his Sabbath preaching and healing claimed him to be, or he was a Sabbath-breaker.

The mission of Jesus is rooted in all the feasts of Judaism. The New Testament describes Jesus not only as Lord of the Sabbath but as the one who fulfills the hopes that all of Israel's feasts express. Throughout history Christians have forgotten their Jewish roots with deadly consequences, both for Judaism and for the integrity of Christianity. When Christians deny their Jewish ancestry, they cut themselves off from the vine in which they live. Judaism is the mother of Christianity, and the Jewish people are the elder brothers and sisters of their younger Christian siblings. Studying the Jewish feasts helps the followers of Jesus understand our rich family heritage.

Reflection and discussion

• Why did Jesus choose to heal people specifically on the Sabbath when he could have chosen any other day?

• What is the danger for Christians to neglect their Jewish heritage?

• How has this study of the feasts of Judaism helped me to better understand the faith of Jesus?

• What is the most important insight I would like to take away from this study of the Jewish feasts?

Prayer

Divine Author of the sacred Scriptures, thank you for the gifts you have given me through the festivals of Israel. Through Jesus, Son of David, teach me the rich heritage that is ours as sons and daughters of Israel. Help me to rejoice and delight in the abundance of your blessings.

SUGGESTIONS FOR FACILITATORS, GROUP SESSION 6

1. Welcome group members and make any final announcements or requests.

2. You may want to pray this prayer as a group:

God of freedom and life, you desire a life of blessing and abundance for all your people. You have given the Sabbath to the world as a weekly reminder of your gift of freedom and a sign of your covenant. As we honor your gift of rest and renewal, help us to remember the blessing of the past and to anticipate your promises for the future. May the regeneration, rededication, and redistribution proclaimed in the biblical Sabbath make us more aware of your desire for justice, compassion, and forgiveness. Send us your Spirit as we study the traditions of our ancestors and bless us with insight and generosity.

3. Ask one or more of the following questions:

- How has this study of the biblical feasts of Judaism helped you appreciate your Christian faith?
- In what way has this study challenged you the most?

4. Discuss lessons 25 through 30. Choose one or more of the questions for reflection and discussion from each lesson to discuss as a group.

5. Ask the group if they would like to study another in the Threshold Bible Study series. Discuss the topic and dates, and make a decision among those interested. Ask the group members to suggest people they would like to invite to participate in the next study series.

6. Ask the group to discuss the insights that stand out most from this study over the past six weeks.

7. Conclude by praying aloud the following prayer or another of your own choosing:

Holy Spirit of the living God, you inspired the writers of the Scriptures and you have guided our study during these weeks. Continue to deepen our love for the word of God in the holy Scriptures and draw us more deeply into the heart of Jesus. We thank you for the hope and assurance you have given us through our understanding of the feasts of Israel. Lead us now to worship and witness more fully and fervently and bless us now and always with the fire of your love.

Ordering Additional Studies

Available Threshold Titles

Eucharist

Angels of God

Pilgrimage in the Footsteps of Jesus

Jerusalem, the Holy City

The Names of Jesus

Advent Light

The Tragic and Triumphant Cross

People of the Passion

The Resurrection and the Life

The Mysteries of the Rosary

The Lamb and the Beasts

The Sacred Heart of Jesus

The Holy Spirit and Spiritual Gifts

Stewardship of the Earth

For a complete description of these and upcoming titles, visit our website at www.ThresholdBibleStudy.com.

For information or orders, visit www.23rdpublications.com or call us at 1-800-321-0411.

Threshold Bible Study is available through your local bookstore or directly from the publisher.